MASTERING RESPECTFUL CONFRONTATION

"Humans have the potential to resolve conflict peacefully—whether it is between individuals or nations. Joe Weston's trainings in Respectful Confrontation show us how to manifest that potential in a way that deepens our wisdom and awakens our heart. Reading this book will bring you more intimacy in your relationships and more capacity to help stem the tide of violence in our world."

– **Tara Brach**, meditation teacher and author of *Radical Acceptance*

"Our globalizing world comes with increasing differences. And with more differences come more conflicts. Joe Weston's *Mastering Respectful Confrontation* teaches better understanding of the other, bringing more freedom, more joy, and easier collaboration. There is nothing more important and inspiring."

– **Jurriaan Kamp**, editor-in-chief, *Ode Magazine*

"Joe Weston has written a very useful book for those activists who believe, as I do, in respect for the humanity of the adversary. The book provides the insights of a keen and sensitive observer of the human condition, but it goes beyond theory and philosophy by providing exercises that integrate respectful practices into daily life."

– **James A. Joseph**, former U.S. ambassador to South Africa, director of the Center for Leadership and Public Values, Duke University

"I have been involved with meditation and other mindfulness practices for over three decades. Yet, in all of my experience, I have never had such focused training on the sometimes harsh realities of human relationships as I had in my training in Respectful Confrontation. What a unique and intensely practical approach to interpersonal communication! My life has been forever changed, and I'm grateful."

– **Tom Goddard,** CEO of Integral Healthcare Solutions,
co-founder of the Integral Institute for Medicine

"We waste precious time in our lives and work stepping around and avoiding difficult situations and conversations. The consequence is distrust and dissatisfaction. The cost can be significant financially, emotionally and spiritually. Joe Weston confronts us with a loving and powerful way to bring authenticity to all our relationships. If you read this book and follow his practices you can be assured that your life will be more productive, profitable, and peaceful."

– **Thomas White,** CEO and founder, The Wisdom Network

"When I first read the word 'confrontation' in Joe Weston's title I believed that it held a negative charge that runs against the grain of my own beliefs. But as I read *Mastering Respectful Confrontation*, I re-framed my view. In fact, I've been waiting for a book like this to come along. Joe offers simple solutions to complex problems in a way that honors the sacredness of the other. Investing time in these practices leads to improved leadership skills, increased profits, and an inspired, productive work environment."

– **Lance Secretan,** corporate leadership consultant and author,
The Spark, the Flame, and the Torch

"Joe Weston is essentially cross-cultural and non-judgmental and equally present with all he meets. His book radiates with the same wisdom, compassion, strength, and understanding."

– **Chaplain Littlejohns,** California State Prison at Jamestown, CA

M A S T E R I N G
RESPECTFUL
CONFRONTATION

BY Joe WESTON

A Guide to Personal Freedom and
Empowered, Collaborative Engagement

MASTERING RESPECTFUL CONFRONTATION:
A Guide to Personal Freedom and Empowered, Collaborative Engagement
By Joe Weston

PUBLISHED BY
Heartwalker Press
4600 Adeline Street, #127 I Emeryville, CA 94608 I (415) 531 7839
www.respectfulconfrontation.com I WWW.JOEWESTON.COM

Names have been changed to protect the identity of private parties.

BOOK COVER / INTERIOR DESIGN   Stefan Hengst, 2K+ Design Inc.
DRAWINGS   David Seiler

COPYRIGHT © 2012 Joe Weston I Printed in the United States

Publisher's Cataloging-in-Publication
(Provided by Quality Books, Inc.)

Weston, Joe, 1964-
    Mastering respectful confrontation: a guide to
personal freedom and empowered, collaborative engagement
/ by Joe Weston.
    p. cm.
    LCCN 2011925973
    ISBN-13: 978-0-9834614-0-1
    ISBN-10: 0-9834614-0-6

    1. Interpersonal confrontation.   I. Title.

BF637.I48W47 2011   158.2
                    QBI11-600080

To my dad, Mel, my mom, Yvette, and my sister, Cori,
my number-one sparring partners in confrontation and conflict,
who taught me the power of dreaming, hard work, and love.

ACKNOWLEDGEMENTS

For as long as I remember, I devoted my life to peace in one form or another. This book is a result of that devotion. I am so appreciative of all the people in my life that helped me to explore and refine the practice of Respectful Confrontation. They include my family, friends, and acquaintances from Queens; all the people and loved ones I've met around the world (who have shown me that my very narrow New York City view of the world is not the only way people see the world), my work and creative colleagues; and my teachers in my studies of theatre and communication, as well as Tai Chi, Buddhism, Taoism, and many of the other mystical traditions, martial arts, and world religions. I am grateful to those who have supported me in healing my anger, sorrow, fear, doubt, and other internal enemies.

I am deeply grateful to all my teachers who encouraged me to question, challenge, and grow. From the bottom of my heart, I acknowledge my teacher, Geshe Sonam Gyaltsen, who has provided me with direction and a strong foundation. Also my dear friends and patient teachers, Harry Faddis, Thirza Dodd, Steve St. Clair, and Jody St. Clair, who continue to remind me that I am never alone and all I really need to do is just be me.

I am most grateful for those who have been a part of the creation of the Respectful Confrontation training. To Jeroen Biegstraaten, Greg John, and Gabriel Clark who helped birth it; to Anna Randall, Manon Romijn, Tom Goddard, and James Dickson who helped to nurture it, as well as La Sarmiento, Leslie Williams, Barbara Wrigley, Terry Shirreffs, Marije Oostindie, Pauline Mudde, Greg Millard, Randy Lind, Lisa Clapier, and the many, many team members and participants around the world. All their efforts have contributed to create a practice that has benefited many.

And a very special acknowledgement to the magical Kristy Lin Billuni, who danced with me so skillfully to get this book finished, and to Simon Warwick-Smith and his team at Warwick Associates for their wisdom and expertise in helping to get it published.

This book is for the generous of heart, the seeker of wisdom, and the truly courageous ones who know that lasting peace is possible. There is nothing more terrifying than to go within and see what is truly there. There is nothing more frightening than to stand across from someone and connect from a place of vulnerability for the sake of positive change. These are the true heroes of our time!

"What a piece of work is a MAN! ~ *and woman*

How noble in REASON, — *common sense*

how infinite in FACULTIES, → *flexible, Skillful means*

in FORM AND MOVING how express and admirable, *True Power*

in ACTION, how like an angel, *creative social activism*

in APPREHENSION, how like a god!" *discernment.*
reflect before acting

— HAMLET, William Shakespeare

[notes in parentheses by Joe Weston]

TABLE OF CONTENTS

INDEX OF EXERCISES

FOREWORD
by Sherrilyn A. Ifill

At the core of every conflict—violent and otherwise—lies the human inability to connect and communicate effectively. In this book, *Mastering Respectful Confrontation*, Joe Weston offers techniques he has learned and perfected over fifteen years to help us engage in productive communication and dialogue.

Weston's timing couldn't be more perfect. A decade into the twenty-first century, the human family remains steeped in conflict, war, crime, and violence. Many have prescribed political, legal, and economic solutions to address our culture of conflict. Certainly, the twentieth century creation of human rights law and values, the movement for democracy in much of the world, the independence of African nations from their former colonial masters, the movement for gender equality and rights in the West, the emergence of protections for child laborers, and the education explosion in many parts of the world have, without question, advanced the prospect of peace and prosperity among many people. But the reality of violence and conflict remains depressingly ever-present with conflicts between countries, within countries, and within communities at an all-time high. These macroconflicts mirror the seemingly unending conflicts between individuals on our jobs, in our communities, in our schools—where violence has become shockingly commonplace—and of course, in our families.

Ironically our conflict-rich society exists at the same time that we are now more focused than human beings have ever been at bettering our personal selves. We study and practice both formal and informal religions. We work out at gyms. We see therapists to help us unlock the secrets of our psyche. We watch Oprah, read self-help books, keep journals in which we track our thoughts and moods, and do yoga. Yet despite all this absorption with our personal selves, we've not come much closer to understanding how to disarm our culture of violence and conflict.

Joe Weston has taken the position that neither the amelioration of external social, political, or economic conditions, nor the elevation of the personal self can alone turn around our deeply conflicted interactions. Instead, Weston argues that we must also learn how to "do conflict"; that is, learn how to engage with those with whom we disagree and with whom we are at odds, so that we can move from conflict to collaboration. Weston does not offer his Respectful Confrontation techniques in an attempt to avoid conflict, or even to judge conflict as something negative.

Conflict is a necessary part of human engagement. It is only when we come to conflict with a closed heart, Weston says, that we create the conditions that escalate conflict to antagonism, hostility, and even violence. The paradox is that our vulnerability and transparency ultimately unleash our greatest power to interact effectively with others.

Any reader of this book should know at the outset that Weston is both ambitious and humble. He doesn't promise that mastering his techniques will keep you from feeling anger, confusion or distress. He doesn't even promise that the faithful use of his techniques will remove conflict from your life. But Weston does challenge each of us to take responsibility for promoting peace in our own lives and in our communities. He asks us to do the hard work of engaging openly and generously with those with whom we may feel the greatest conflict. This is the work of peace-making. And we can all do it.

SHERRILYN A. IFILL *is a civil rights attorney, professor of law at the University of Maryland School of Law, and author of* On The Courthouse Lawn: Confronting the Legacy of Lynching in the Twenty-first Century.

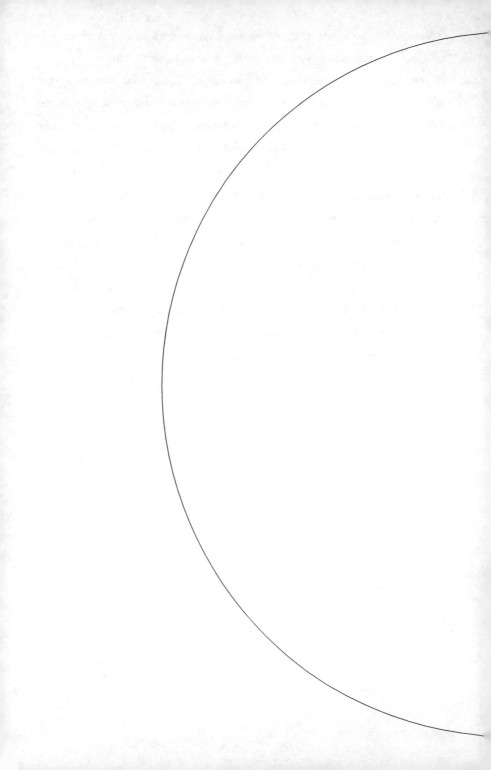

INTRODUCING
RESPECTFUL CONFRONTATION

"We have to face the fact that either all of us are going to die together or we are going to learn to live together, and if we are to live together, we have to talk."

— Eleanor Roosevelt

INTRODUCTION

At the heart of Respectful Confrontation is the belief that it is possible to stand in your power, speak your truth, hear the truth of others, and get your needs met in a way that won't harm you or others. Many of us have negative associations with confrontation; we think it is the same as conflict. However, by exploring the principles and exercises in this book, you will discover that confrontation is nothing more than open-hearted engagement and ultimately the most effective way to avoid and resolve conflict.

I've been involved with this for fifteen years and yet I still am astonished by the impact it has. People with relationship difficulties have permanent breakthroughs, and those in the work environment tackle difficult conflicts with bosses, employees, and colleagues. Even those who solve problems professionally, like mediators and negotiators, have positive results with these methods. For some, this practice is a way to enhance communication skills and for others, an inner journey of self-awareness and liberation.

Here's how one couple was affected:

"I attended one of Joe's Respectful Confrontation weekends, and it had a huge impact. Firstly, I really learned *how* to respectfully confront people. We didn't just talk about it. I've used that recently with business vendors and colleagues who owed me money, and it was immensely useful. When my wife and I returned, it changed how she worked as a therapist; she started using some of the approaches learned from Joe.

Also, we've been married for twenty-five years and we get in a rut. Somehow, the exercises opened us up emotionally and we reconnected and enjoyed a dramatically revamped relationship. It was an invigorating effect. It is a big deal to be able to reaffirm and connect more deeply with someone you love, when you haven't been doing as good a job relating as you might want to. It is all in understanding Joe's framework and then *doing* the exercises."

If this interests you, keep reading to find out how. When you master Respectful Confrontation, you will have the ability to solve problems, overcome personal challenges, feel empowered to live the life you choose, and support others in doing the same.

MOTIVATION

Why, even though we know better, do we continue to play out the same dramas with our families, friends, colleagues, and acquaintances? On a global scale, why do we struggle to end war, strife, and injustice even with advanced technology, abundance of resources, easy access to information, and international interdependence?

These questions have inspired me to form the theory and practice of Respectful Confrontation. Throughout my life, I have wrestled with these questions in various contexts. I have worked with the Dutch consulate, political refugees from the Balkans, and inmates at a California prison. I have studied martial arts, Buddhism, Taoism, the teachings of Jesus, and other spiritual traditions. I have trained corporate and non-profit employees from every continent, and worked with social activists, artists, middle school children, teachers, and parents.

After many years, I made a number of discoveries revealing some reasons why we resist change to our old, destructive patterns and the creation of lasting, positive change. **These reasons are:**

- *Most of us still operate with old beliefs and systems that don't currently serve us. Until we shift our paradigms around power, confrontation/conflict, and assertiveness/aggression, we will continue to spiral back to old, ineffective ways of addressing problems*

- *Most of us lack a vital depth of self-reflection. Good at judging others, we forget to evaluate our own actions to see how we contribute to the problem*

- *Most of us don't see that our individual actions have a strong impact on the whole, with others, society, and globally. We must acknowledge our aggressive behavior to overcome its negative impact*

- *Most of us don't trust the power that love, compassion, and open-hearted connection can have in our personal lives and on a global scale. Therefore, we don't feel confident to engage with others that we don't recognize, nor do we take the time to work out problems before they escalate into conflict*

- *Most of us see our unique viewpoints and beliefs as the absolute truth*

And yet, no matter where I have been in the world, I have seen clearly that despite our cultural, racial, national, and religious differences, we share common desires. Likewise, each individual on the planet has a unique and interesting story to tell.

When I realized that every person I encountered had, like me, the same desire for happiness, for freedom from suffering, and for understanding, I could connect with each person's humanity. We overcame our differences and found a way to engage with respect and creativity, even if we had different viewpoints.

Overcoming differences, in order to engage in authentic relations required a lot of effort, including the process of consciously taking responsibility for my own behavior, setting aside my judgments, and choosing to stay engaged with others who were often very challenging. I could only imagine how frustrating, frightening, and seemingly impossible it would be for others. These potential obstacles are why I have spent more than fifteen years culling my learning and experience to create a training that would support others on their quest to find answers to these questions.

The purpose of this training is to empower others to:
- *Overcome personal obstacles*
- *Open to deeper levels of personal freedom, inner peace, and fulfillment*
- *Walk through life from a place of power, asserting in a positive way*
- *Improve efficacy and influence at work*
- *Increase trust, improve communication, limit misunderstandings, and avoid and resolve conflict*
- *Shift and reframe views on true power, confrontation / conflict, and assertiveness / aggression*
- *Engage with others in order to bridge the gaps of personal, cultural,*

and societal separation—to deepen connections, bring individuals closer together, and to empower all involved

- Seek out collaboration to solve personal and community problems

This book is an overview of the theories and practices of this training.

CONTEXT

Imagine a world where each individual had the commitment and the skill to positively interact with all beings with respect and honor even if the others' views and beliefs were different. Imagine a world where we learn how to engage with such respect and honor. Imagine being committed to collaboration and not breaking the connection through fear, hate or anger. Imagine avoiding further misunderstandings and, ultimately, fights, crime, and war. Imagine feeling so fulfilled and confident in yourself that you naturally feel the desire to empower others.

The essence of Respectful Confrontation, whether confronting oneself or others, is to speak what needs to be spoken even if it is uncomfortable. *The most effective way to avoid and resolve conflict is with confrontation!*

Conflict can only occur when we are being negatively judgmental and acting from our reactive behavior—when the goal of a relationship or an encounter is to defeat the other or when someone chooses to avoid hearing or speaking the truth. These behaviors break down contact and the clear lines of communication. Ultimately, conflict arises when communication is no longer clear and open.

I believe negative judgment is the underlying cause of most conflict. By negatively judging or labeling something, we create separation. For example, walk down a busy street and notice how quickly you label and judge the people you see based on social class, skin color or political affiliation. As soon as we put other people into a convenient category, we give ourselves permission to avoid getting to know them. We see them from the perspective of our assumptions, which probably has nothing to do with who they are! This behavior is common.

Such common behavior may not seem so severe at first, but this kind of relating to the world slowly leads to a chronic lack of connection. We shut our hearts to one another and no longer concern ourselves with what others are going through; they simply become statistics to us. Jesus said, "Stop judging by mere appearances and make a right judgment."

We have moved into an age of global connection. There is little on this planet that doesn't in some way affect something else; every altercation has ramifications to all nations. When the economy or government of one nation shifts, ripples will eventually reach other nations. The news is filled with stories showing the volatility of the world economy and the urgency to heal our relationship with the environment.

Through the Internet and the media, we can instantly find any kind of information, and we can connect with anyone, anywhere within seconds. With tools like Facebook, Twitter, Internet chatting, and sophisticated mobile phones, our most intimate facets are exposed for all to see. We have really become one global community—all part of an intricate web.

Remember the student uprising in Iran in 2009? The Iranian government tried very hard to keep the news from getting out. But with the use of mobile phones, the world witnessed the chaos and watched Neda Soltan, the "Angel of Freedom", bleed to death after being beaten in the streets of Tehran.

We are currently in a phase of history where much is shifting, even crumbling. This has enormous advantages. This means we discard old, outdated ways to make room for new modes of governing and relating to one another. This time also contains the possibility to cause havoc if we are not responsible. This shift requires us to be more involved with the whole.

In October 2008, Alan Greenspan, former chairman of the U.S. Federal Reserve Board, shook the international financial market when he admitted at a United States Senate hearing that his theories on regulations were flawed and acknowledged that he had put too much faith in the self-correcting power of free markets. The world suffered from the damaging effects of greed and principles based on profiting from the loss of others.

Notice how many issues arise to ask us to take action, not only for ourselves and our families, but for all beings. How uplifting to recall the number of citizens around the world who supported the victims of the Tsunami of 2004 and who raised an estimated $1.8 billion for recovery efforts. Additionally, the over $3 billion raised for the earthquake in Haiti reflects this global support. In the current economic crisis, we see reports of neighbors organizing food drives and raising money for families who are losing their homes or who can't afford health insurance.

"What we need in the United States is not division;

what we need in the United States is not hatred;

what we need in the United States is not violence and lawlessness,

but is love and wisdom, and compassion toward one another,

and a feeling of justice toward those who still suffer

within our country."

— **Robert F. Kennedy**

WHY RESPECTFUL CONFRONTATION?

If we are going to move peacefully through the current shifts in our personal relationships, in our communities, and on a global scale, we will need to develop clear, respectful ways to communicate in order to find new, creative solutions to existing problems. Unfortunately, many of us have not been taught the language and skills of collaboration. Respectful Confrontation is an ideal mode of communication that enables us to stay connected and engaged, and to confront one another on both loving and hurtful issues.

The twenty-first century is the era of personal responsibility to a greater cause. We have progressed from a period of self-discovery and self-development, especially in the more technologically advanced countries. The 1960s and 1970s allowed us to break away from old ideas and open to more expanded views of the world and individual freedom. The 1980s and 1990s gave us the opportunity to work on ourselves and to begin the journey of self-revelation and healing.

This has created a culture where words like *karma* have become a part of our everyday vocabulary. We understand very well that our actions have consequences, and that we have the power and the right to transform and evolve. We see the potential of the individual and have created a culture where many of us have the freedom to attempt to manifest our goals.

For those of us who are fortunate enough to have this opportunity, *I say now is the time to take what we have learned and do something with this knowledge!* We have the resources, skills, healing, and wisdom to actually make a difference in our relationships, in the workplace, in our neighborhoods, and globally. Every small contribution makes a difference. If we can truly take responsibility for our actions and support others in their process toward conscious interaction, we will see positive change.

Peacemaking should not focus solely on law enforcement and getting armies to put down their weapons. The true work of peacemaking is teaching each individual how to shift his or her personal behavior when engaging with others. For positive, lasting change to occur, we must develop the skills to stay engaged with others in a peaceful way, even when we disagree and especially when someone has been hurt.

The true practice of the peacemaker is to manage reactive behavior while having the generosity to hear someone else's side to a story and then skillfully reach resolution or find ways to disagree respectfully. This is the blueprint of a twenty-first century peacemaking coalition.

And it all starts with the individual! It doesn't take place on the battlefields. It takes place in the family kitchens, the schoolyard, the workplace, and in line at the supermarket. Each time we avoid or resolve conflict we move one step closer to a culture of lasting peace. Disturbing feelings and misunderstandings may still be present, but we will feel confident that we can overcome these disturbances and find a way to stay connected.

SIMPLE SOLUTIONS

The practice of the peacemaker is an important premise. The problems may never go away, *but how we deal with the problems must change.* This is hard work. It's difficult enough to maintain engagement and avoid arguments with people we know and with whom we share common beliefs, values, language, background, and history. Imagine when we have to engage with others who have different beliefs, lifestyles, religions, and languages. The more we understand what causes separation, the easier it will be to avoid conflict and stay in healthy, open engagement leading to deeper levels of intimacy, and more efficacy in work and in collaboration.

The antidote to separation is curiosity. It's that simple. When you find yourself shutting your heart to someone or creating distance, see if you can muster up the curiosity to get to know him or her. Engage in an openhearted way with Respectful Confrontation. You don't have to agree, nor do you have to adopt the other person's philosophies, but what you can do is try to understand alternative viewpoints. Just this simple exercise will instantly change your life and also change the world.

This process starts with you getting out of your intellect—the part of you that only approaches the world from a place of statistics, race, and social status—and getting back to a place where you engage from your heart. From your heart, you can develop compassion and understanding, which leads to action and change.

Yes, we need our intellect to process and analyze. It is impressive how far our intelligence has taken us with technological advances.

We have so many resources at our fingertips. We are capable of gazing deeply into space and also probing the smallest of particles. If intellect were enough to solve our problems, we would already have eliminated personal arguments, crime, and hunger. Martin Luther King, Jr. said, "We have guided missiles and misguided men."

We won't take action until we *feel* what is happening around us. When you are fully in your heart and feeling compassion, you will not be able to tolerate that people are hungry, that you are fighting with loved ones, or that others are suffering. You will search for new policies and strategies that acknowledge that the only way *you* can win is if everyone else involved also wins.

There are those who say my ideas are naïve. They say our problems are far too complicated to be solved with love, compassion, and openhearted connection. I guess it all depends on how you view love, compassion, and openhearted connection. If you see them as soft and weak, the policies of hippies running in the fields with flowers in their hair, then, yes, that will never resolve our serious problems.

I say those who are attached to the current paradigm are the ones who are naïve. They keep using the same, complicated means to try to overcome complicated problems. They keep arguing and fighting, and they are not getting any closer to solutions. They still believe that war is a way to eliminate war. I can't think of anything more naïve. The concept is absurd. Nations have been trying it for millennia, and it just hasn't worked.

How many wars have we had since World War I, "the war to end all wars" that ended in 1918? The Dalai Lama said, "Using war to eliminate war is like using fire to put out a fire." And Martin Luther King, Jr. said, "Darkness cannot drive out darkness: only light can do that. Hate cannot drive out hate: only love can do that." It's time to try something else.

My response to the skeptics is this: the problems may be complicated, but the solutions need to be simple. Albert Einstein said, "You cannot solve a problem from the same consciousness that created it. You must see the world anew." Using complicated methods to solve problems only creates more complications. Begin with first acknowledging the power of openhearted connection, which includes respect, compassion, generosity, and understanding. Then, learn the skills to engage from the heart and maintain that connection with others, even when it gets challenging. *When you are in your heart you tap into your wisdom and common sense as a source of energy and power.*

But this is not easy! So, let's look at it this way: the problems are complicated, the solutions are simple, and implementing the solutions is hard work. There's the rub: *the reason why, even though we know better, we still have conflict on a personal and global level is because the simple solutions are hard to implement.*

The solution lies in learning and practicing a mode of communication that fosters clarity, understanding, respect, and collaboration. Respectful Confrontation, in its purest state, is simply openhearted engagement. Judgments, assumptions, and all the concepts that keep us separate seem to fall away. You begin to feel what vulnerability really is, and more importantly, you begin to discover the enormous power in vulnerability And I believe that *it is only in your vulnerability that your true power is revealed.*

From this openhearted state, it is possible to walk through life from a place of power. Asserting yourself in a positive way allows you to deal with issues confidently and effectively to create a life of fulfillment and freedom while empowering others. You naturally deepen connections and avoid and resolve conflict to create collaboration.

Although there are people in the world who have a lot of love, compassion, and wisdom, it is not enough just to have these qualities. I know many loving, compassionate, and wise people who still complain that they wish they could be doing more to help others. They are unhappy with how they live their lives and often find themselves in repeated cycles of arguments and relationship problems. What is required is a training to learn the skills to put these innate talents to use in a productive, focused, and efficient way. Rochelle, an IT manager and an advocate for peace, said, "Through Respectful Confrontation I have discovered that peaceful doesn't mean passive. Thank you for helping me to find the voice I thought was dead."

Is it possible to have this openhearted connection all the time? For some people this is possible. If this is you, go for it! Join the ranks of Mahatma Gandhi, Martin Luther King, Jr., and Mother Theresa and live out your purpose. If you are like me, this openhearted state doesn't happen all the time. That's why we need a method to practice!

You may be thinking, "No way! I'm not going to walk around with my heart totally open. I will get hurt, used or abused." I think this reflection is very smart. It would not be of benefit to anyone, especially you, to be that open. Having an openhearted engagement doesn't mean you should always be totally open.

But there are not just two switches on your heart: "open" and "close". These practices will help you develop a more intricate "switchboard" or "dimmer switch" when engaging with others to provide you with more options, plus the speed and agility to switch instantly. What this means is that it is possible to be open, but every interaction requires you to always discern and then adjust how open you should be.

Openhearted connection on its own is not enough. We need a way to combine this with wisdom, strength, courage, and a warrior approach to peace. So I use the metaphor of martial arts as an important foundation for Respectful Confrontation. The true martial arts master embodies all the attributes of a warrior combined with wisdom and compassion.

MASTERING RESPECTFUL CONFRONTATION

MARTIAL ARTS AS METAPHOR

Growing up as a boy on the streets of New York City meant a lot of useless fighting. It was normal for my friends and me to fight with other kids in the neighborhood and even with each other. And the fights were never really about anything important.

My dad, who also grew up on the streets of New York City, came from a world where you had to fight and hang out with the tough guys in order to assert any sense of power. This resulted in him spending some time in prison when I was a boy.

I quickly realized that this was not my world. I saw how silly it was. It didn't make sense to me. I often thought, *why are we fighting so much? It's not leading us anywhere! There must be a better way to deal with our differences. We could be doing so many more fun and constructive things than wasting our time fighting!* So I stopped fighting.

These reflections didn't go over well with my friends and certainly not with my dad. What was a man who based his whole strategy of survival on fighting going to do with a son who wouldn't fight? What would my friends do with someone who wouldn't keep up the game of alliances and opponents? I found them pulling away from me and me from them.

My dad did his best. He tried anything to "toughen me up." He kept teaching me how to fight, hoping I'd change, but I was seen as a weakling. I fell into the group of boys who, according to American society, would never know what it means to be a powerful man. I stood on the sidelines and watched the "Rambo" types get ahead in our "nice guys finish last" culture.

Behind my "nice guy" smile I was very withdrawn and found it hard to speak my truth. It was hard for me to connect with others. I walked around feeling that everyone was out to get me. The only feelings I expressed were anger and frustration.

Then, in my twenties, I decided to take a Tai Chi class. Through the process of learning the form and philosophies of Tai Chi, I developed self-confidence and a new way to engage with the world. I felt confident about asserting myself without causing harm to myself or to others. I went on to study other forms of martial arts and learned discipline, strength training, and skillful fighting techniques. I also discovered a strong emphasis on respect, commitment to personal responsibility, and self-improvement along with a desire to engage with others in a peaceful way.

The more I developed my martial arts skills, the less defensive and fearful I was. That made me less prone to violence. Doesn't this make sense? By learning how to fight in an honorable way I discovered that I could take care of myself without having to fight!

Stephen Hayes, who is an American Ninja master who brought the art to the United States, and was a bodyguard to the Dalai Lama, emphasizes that the point of learning how to fight is to ultimately have the skills to avoid fighting. Lao Tzu, considered by many to be the father of Taoism, said, "A good warrior is never violent. A good fighter is never offensive. A great victor defeats an opponent, but not by challenging. A great commander is humble. This is called the power of non-contention. To follow this path is to follow the pattern of the subtle law of the universe."

Take a look at history, or your own personal life, and you will see that many of our arguments and wars occurred when an individual or group felt that they were defenseless or powerless.

The Cold War of the late twentieth century is a perfect example. Leaders in the United States and the Soviet Union, after World War II, were in very powerful positions and realized they had a lot to lose. This imbalance of power led to a deep, innate fear that they couldn't protect all they had acquired and a sense that there would always be a threat from the outside. Both nations invested time and money into building defense systems, nuclear bombs, and spy strategies. Just look at all the propaganda in the press, films, and TV designed to generate fear and mistrust.

How many movies were made in the 1950s about invaders from space? Look at the amount of valuable resources and the threat to the survival of the planet this mentality caused! Even though we don't hear much about it in the news these days, we have enough nuclear bombs on the planet to kill each human being fifty to sixty times.

A martial arts practice creates a feeling of security from within because you can actually protect yourself. When the world seems less threatening, you are more prone to open your heart, engage with others in a confident way, and actually feel the urge to support others during their personal challenges.

Coming back to Respectful Confrontation as a practice, you will become a skilled, confident communicator, engaging effortlessly in all situations, both loving and aggressive, with compassion and personal power.

Even though we will talk about punching, kicking, and blocking in the traditional sense of fighting as a way to illustrate communication, Respectful Confrontation is not a fighting technique. The encounters are in the realm of communication and human interaction, where awareness, feelings, needs, thoughts, personal boundaries, and relationships come into play. Your "battlefield" is the kitchen table, the water cooler at work, and the supermarket, where everyone you encounter is your sparring partner. Every interaction you have is an opportunity to put your skills to good use to engage in a way that is respectful and openhearted, where nobody gets hurt, and where all feel empowered because they have been heard.

"Courage is what it takes to stand up and speak.
Courage is also what it takes to sit down and listen."

— **Winston Churchill**

GETTING STARTED

In this book you will practice techniques to:

- *Expand your view of your own personal power*
- *Delve deeply into the workings of communication and how you engage with others*
- *Examine closely what the differences are between confrontation and conflict*
- *Identify assertiveness and aggression*
- *Learn effective skills and tools for engaging in both loving and aggressive situations*

Respectful Confrontation is broken down into four parts, each one exploring a different aspect of the skills for successfully engaging with others in an openhearted and empowered way.

....

▸ **THE PRACTICE OF DEVELOPING THE RESPECTFUL SELF**

Here, I will review what is needed before you engage with others to develop mindfulness, courage, confidence, and endurance. This includes developing respect, personal motivation, courageous self-reflection, presence, centeredness, and true power.

....

▸ **THE PRACTICE OF RESPECTFUL ENGAGEMENT**

In this section you will build an understanding of the intricate working of communication and the differences between confrontation and conflict. You'll gain proficiency in the language of the body (such as feelings, needs, and intuition), and effectively make contact with others.

....

▸ **THE PRACTICE OF RESPECTFUL OFFENSE**

This part explores tools to deepen contact, speak and hear truth, overcome barriers to connection, honor personal space, explore the dance of giving and receiving, and understand the power of assertiveness in creating positive change and empowering others.

....

▸ **THE PRACTICE OF RESPECTFUL DEFENSE**

Finally, I will examine the formidable obstacles to collaborative engagement. I offer strategies to stay engaged and get to the heart of an issue without destructive or conflicting results. These obstacles include all the unspoken, unexamined patterns that keep you from speaking your truth and listening to another's point of view. This is called aggression, violence or "unconscious reactive behavior".

Along with principles and exercises, each section contains the following:

(🧑) **At the beginning of each section,** a **DIALOGUE** called *"The Dilemma"* that illustrates our common challenges and mistakes with communication and how we get it wrong.

(❞) **At the beginning of each chapter,** a **QUOTE** from a real-life participant from past workshops and trainings.

(🧑) **At the end of each section,** an **EXAMPLE** of a Respectful Confrontation, demonstrating how the practices of that section successfully enhance communication and help to get it right;

(✎) a **TRUE STORY** of a participant who has benefited from the practice;

(✓) and a **SUMMARY** of key points and topics in that section.

HOW TO USE THIS BOOK

You may choose to read this book without doing the exercises. You will receive some useful insights and theory and still notice a shift in how you engage with yourself and others. These teachings, however, are meant to be practiced and integrated into your life. Explore with the body, with the heart, and with the emotions as well as with the mind. **Here are some tips and terminology to help get you started:**

MAKE IT PERSONAL

The more you can personalize this material, the more it will impact you. Connect the principles, stories, struggles, and triumphs to your own life. When reading about the practices and the exercises, take the time to stop and really try them. Look at yourself in a truthful way—even if you don't like what you see!

Throughout the book, I present the challenges we *all* face with the various aspects of Respectful Confrontation. As I suggest solutions, I offer tools and techniques that *you* can practice to overcome these challenges. Also, when I use the third person, implying that *he* or *she* is either powerful or aggressive (or skillful or unfair), I try my best to keep it as balanced as possible in order to avoid typical stereotypes and assumptions.

I don't expect you to take everything I say with blind faith. Read this as a discussion between the two of us. Stay open to contemplate the theories and to experience the exercises as a way to get a deeper sense of this process. Try it before you draw your conclusions.

Examine the information I offer from all sides and use healthy criticism. See what it means to you and if it has a place in your life. You may already know some of the theories and exercises, but I recommend you practice them as if you are experiencing them for the first time. Even though you know them, you have never experienced them within the context of Respectful Confrontation. Be open to new discoveries.

CREATE A SAFE ENVIRONMENT

Begin with reading the theory and then take a few days or even a few weeks to explore the exercises that follow. There is no need to rush through this process. Like any path, you could see this as a journey of self-discovery and self-empowerment. *You are learning a practice.*

Do the exercise in a private space where you will not disturb others. A quiet room with little clutter where you are free to move and make sounds is ideal. If you practice the methods in your daily life, do so with others who understand that you are trying out new techniques and will understand that you may not get it right the first time.

You may also choose to go through this process with a group of friends. That is a fabulous way to experience the work, get direct feedback from others, and help you stay on track. If you work with a group, be sure to talk beforehand about setting clear goals, making up a schedule (how many sessions, days, and times), finding an appropriate location, establishing how you run the sessions, who is taking on the role of facilitator for each session, and how you plan to communicate with each other and give feedback.

Get a separate journal or workbook to take notes, do the exercises, and journal on how you are seeing this work manifesting in your life.

PRACTICE THE EXERCISES

The exercises in this book are designed to help you develop your ability to access your innate wisdom and master the practice of Respectful Confrontation. As you connect with deeper aspects of yourself, you will tap into a wealth of knowledge and energy. You will find that a more consistent connection to the wisdom of your heart and body will lead to more self-confidence, courage, and success in your communication and life goals.

When you get to an exercise, read through it a few times before you practice it in order to get an understanding of each step. When you actually practice the exercise, go to Appendix Two on page 285 and find an outline of the exercise. This will help you to stay on track with each step of the process. Have the book close by so you can refer back to the steps or you can ask someone to read it out loud to you while you go through the process.

Every exercise begins with the same preliminary steps and closing steps. You will find a clear explanation and outline of these preliminary and closing steps in Appendix One on page 281.

There is no need to do the exercises "right"; especially the first time you try them. The best way to approach this work is to be curious about each exercise and see how you can make it work for you. You are better off assessing and evaluating how you did as opposed to judging yourself and worrying if you failed or succeeded. The former leads to constructive progress and the latter stifles growth. Remember, this is a lifelong process. I assure you that if you learn the language, do the exercises, and apply them in your life, you will be transformed.

SOME USEFUL TERMS

As well as helping us develop deeper levels of understanding, words can move us into action, stir up feelings, bring us closer together, and also cause arguments and strife. In this book, I use words that are loaded with prejudice, fear, emotion, and history. If you get triggered by these terms, take the opportunity to examine deep feelings and question some of your beliefs and viewpoints.

When you take the time to get to the heart of what someone is saying, you learn more about who they are and you cut down on misunderstanding. Remember, the words may help you understand and clarify but Respectful Confrontation is more about the experience. Communication is an experience, not just a concept.

 Here are some terms used often in this book and how I use them in the context of Respectful Confrontation:

AGGRESSION

Any behavior, action, remark, gesture or facial expression that impacts another with the goal to disempower, and/or is received by the other in a harmful, threatening way.

ASSERTIVENESS

Any behavior, action, remark, gesture or facial expression that impacts another with the goal to empower, and/or is received by the other in a positive way.

COMPASSION

The desire for others to be free from suffering and subsequently acting on that desire.

CONFLICT

An encounter that leads to the further separation of individuals, the breakdown of relationship, and the disempowerment of the other.

CONFRONTATION

An encounter that leads to individuals coming closer together, deepening relationship, and the empowerment of all involved.

LOVE

The desire for others to be happy and subsequently acting on that desire.

MINDFULNESS

Staying alert to one's thoughts, words, and actions to ensure having a positive, healthy impact on self, others or the surroundings, and to avoid having a negative, harmful impact on self, others or the surroundings.

OPENHEARTED CONNECTION

Engaging with others (strangers, friends or adversaries) with compassion, understanding, and respect, as well as having the courage and skill to speak and hear the truth of everyone involved without getting harmed or harming others.

REACTIVE BEHAVIOR

Any thoughts, words or actions that are not done mindfully, usually coming from disturbing emotions and habitual, unexamined patterns learned from childhood causing misunderstanding and conflict. This usually occurs unconsciously as a way to avoid confrontation, intimacy, growth, and speaking and hearing the truth.

TRUE POWER

Possessing an equal mastery of grounding, focus, strength, and flexibility; engaging with vulnerability instead of brute force.

VIOLENCE

Any behavior, action, remark, gesture or facial expression that harms oneself or another, either physically or emotionally. This includes all types of aggression from outward acts, like muggings and bombs, to passive-aggressive or reactive behavior, like gossip and not returning phone calls.

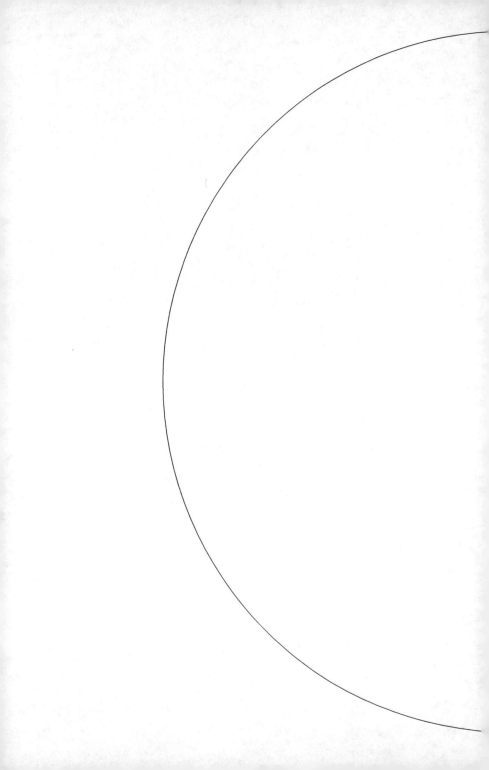

THE PRACTICE OF
RESPECTFUL CONFRONTATION

"Your vision will become clear only when you look into your heart. Who looks outside, dreams. Who looks inside, awakens."

— Carl Jung

THE CORE EXERCISE:
OPENHEARTED INTERACTION

Before I break down the different aspects of this process, I will introduce an exercise that sums up the whole practice. It is simple, but within it is contained all the wisdom and power of Respectful Confrontation. If you can master this exercise, then you have achieved an important goal that will lead to personal freedom, fulfillment, and empowered, collaborative engagement. Exercises, like this one, which open you to deeper levels of self-awareness, can change the quality of your life in a powerful and beneficial way. Read it through a couple of times before you continue with the rest of the practice.

THE CORE EXERCISE
OPENHEARTED INTERACTION

▶ **Choose a good time and location**

Do this exercise when you are alone or around people who can respect your need for focus and silence. Find a place to do this where there is enough space around you.

▶ **Start with the basic sitting pose**

Sit in a comfortable way. Your spine should be vertical and relaxed (either sitting on a pillow on the floor with legs crossed or sitting at the edge of a chair with feet flat on the floor); your breath should be relaxed, steady, and deep; your eyes closed or partially closed, looking down towards the ground; your shoulders and jaw relaxed, and your hands resting on your knees or in your lap. (See illustration on page 281)

▶ **Bring your attention to your center**

Take a moment to imagine a spot that is about three finger-widths below your navel, somewhere in the center of your lower belly. Try to see this point with your mind's eye and focus on it for a period of time. (See illustration on page 282)

MASTERING RESPECTFUL CONFRONTATION

▸ **Place all of your attention on your breath**

From your center become aware of your breath. This simple task helps you to come into alignment with yourself and into the present. There is no need to change your breath. Simply notice it.

▸ **Become aware of your physical body**

What sensations are you aware of from your center? Exhaustion? Hunger? Tension? Pleasure? There's no need to change anything. All sensations, even the unpleasant ones, are welcome.

▸ **Become aware of your emotional body**

What emotions are you aware of? Excitement? Fear? Boredom? Joy? Anger? Sorrow? All feelings are welcome, even the ones that are often seen as unpleasant. There is no need to fix them.

▸ **Become aware of your mental body**

From your center, what thoughts are most present right now? Are your thoughts open and expansive or tight and judgmental? Don't try to control your thoughts, just let them flow by.

▸ **Become aware of your surroundings**

From your center, become aware of the space that you are in right now. Keep your eyes closed. Do you notice sounds? Air temperature? Smells? Can you feel furniture or movement? If you are outside, do you feel the trees, the wind? Place yourself in this space, in this context, at this moment. What is your relationship with this space? Let yourself be influenced by your surroundings.

▸ **Become aware of others**

Now focus on your heart or the middle of your chest. From that place, notice how connected you feel to something larger than you, to the very essence that unites all beings and all phenomena. You may not feel much connection or you may feel a lot. Don't judge your connection, simply notice it.

Now see if you can sense how connected you feel right now to all beings on this planet. Understand that this connection changes from moment to moment. How connected are you to your loved ones and those you know and feel close to in life? How connected in your heart do you feel to strangers and possible adversaries? Now notice how all of these connections influence you at this moment.

If you are doing this exercise in a space with other people, try opening your awareness to the others in the room. Keep your eyes closed and see if it is possible to connect with the others who are present. Not with touch or sounds but simply with your awareness. How does that feel?

▸ **Draw this feeling into your heart with some deep breaths**

With a stronger connection to yourself, to your surroundings, and to others, take a couple of big, deep breaths and give yourself permission to feel this experience. Feel it in your heart. Let yourself experience whatever comes up.

▸ **Slowly open your eyes and connect with your surroundings and others**

Keep breathing, open your eyes, and continue to feel your connection with yourself, your surroundings, and with others. Whether you are doing this on your own or with a group, become aware of the reactions that arise. You may want to laugh. Good, do it. You may feel fear or excitement or sadness. Great. Let yourself feel it.

If you are doing this exercise with others around you, seek out eye contact. Try to stay connected to anyone with whom you make eye contact for a moment. Really notice what happens if you make a heart connection with this person. Ask yourself, *how am I impacting this person at this moment and how are they impacting me?*

Notice that you may want to put up a mask or censor your feelings. Try to stay as openhearted as you were when your eyes were closed. If this makes you nervous or uncomfortable, or if you feel resistance, then give yourself the space to feel that reaction.

▸ **Shake out and stretch your legs**

Stretch and shake out any tension you have acquired. You may not be doing a lot of movement, but this exercise requires a lot of exertion and energy.

▸ **Make notes on what you have discovered**

In order to see your progress and learn from this practice, make some notes. Don't judge yourself, just evaluate. Write down how it went and what happened. Did you learn anything new? Did you come across a new challenge? Are you seeing yourself in a new way? Make a note about how you will approach the exercise next time.

▸ **Follow the recommended schedule**

In the beginning you should give yourself fifteen to thirty minutes for this exercise. Start with doing it at least three times a week. As you get more familiar with it, you will be able to do the whole exercise in five to fifteen minutes. You have perfected this exercise when you find that you are always walking through life with an openhearted connection and full awareness of your whole self, your surroundings, those around you, and the planet.

This exercise helps you to feel the power of openhearted connection and the benefits of being more aware of others, your surroundings, and even yourself, resulting in:

- *Realizing your goals and creating a life of fulfillment and creative freedom*
- *Deepening wisdom and tapping into your innate power*
- *Having a bigger impact and more influence with others*
- *Limiting misunderstandings and conflict and avoiding harm and hurting others*
- *Heightening the ability to listen in order to create the foundation for collaborative, empowered engagement and generate more cooperation, respect, and understanding*

This exercise shines a light beam, piercing the confusion and darkness of communication, to support us on the path toward true freedom. Now let's put that light beam through a prism and look at all the refracted aspects that make up the practice and theory of Respectful Confrontation.

THE PRACTICE OF
DEVELOPING
THE RESPECTFUL SELF

MASTERING RESPECTFUL CONFRONTATION

THE DILEMMA

EMPLOYEE   Mr. Jackson?

MANAGER   Yes?

EMPLOYEE   I'm here for our meeting.

MANAGER   What meeting?

EMPLOYEE   You said we could talk about my raise?

MANAGER   Oh, yeah. Well, this is not a good time. I have a deadline. Let's do it next week.

EMPLOYEE   Oh, okay.

MANAGER   And while you are here, I have some last minute things that need to get done ASAP. Why don't you make a list?

EMPLOYEE   Oh, okay.

"

"For so long, I saw myself as the victim. I wasn't living my life. Life was living me. Through Respectful Confrontation, I now see how I contribute to my own unhappiness. I am looking at aspects of myself I have avoided. I actually feel happy. Who would have thought that the one person I needed to confront the most was me!"

"

COURAGEOUS
SELF-REFLECTION

The first part of the practice focuses on the development of the respectful, responsible, and powerful self.

Throughout history, most martial arts were practiced as a way to alleviate violence, as well as being a spiritual practice, and a path to self-realization. Morihei Ueshiba, founder of the martial art Aikido, said, "The purpose of training is to tighten up the slack, toughen the body, and polish the spirit." This challenging path is an inward journey and one of deep contemplation, skill, endurance, and courage.

Ueshiba goes on to say, "There are no contests in the Art of Peace. Defeat means to defeat the mind of contention that we harbor within." There are many accounts of great teachers encouraging their students to embark on the path within. According to Buddhism and other Eastern philosophies, the state of enlightenment, or liberation, is already a part of your consciousness. It is up to you to find it within the depths of your mind. Buddha said, "Look within. Be still. Free from fear and attachment. Know the sweet joy of living in the way." Similarly, Jesus said: "Neither shall they say, lo here! Or, lo there! For, behold, the Kingdom of God is within you."

To overcome your own internal enemies, like fear, hate, anger, grief, jealousy, violence, prejudice, and confusion, is viewed by many to be the true noble fight. Not everyone is ready for this path within. Most of us give up, get frightened or get bored to name a few possibilities. This is further reiterated by Angel Kyodo Williams, a contemporary, innovative, spiritual activist and author of books like "Being Black: Zen and the Art of Living with Fearlessness and Grace," who says, "The most frightening thing people can do is to take an honest look at themselves and see themselves in a truthful way."

On this sacred journey, you come across parts of yourself that you'd rather not see and feel or parts that have been conveniently buried or suppressed. It is a painful process to see all of you—the pleasant parts and the less pleasant parts. Courageous Self-Reflection brings these parts out into the light. When you see these hidden parts, you actually see that some of them are not so bad or scary. They are actually very interesting!

Think about it. If you only present the "nice" parts of you, you become very shallow, flat, and boring. Think of a painter and her palette of colors. If she only uses colors like pink, light yellow, and light blue, then she is limited to creating nice and simple art. Imagine a palette that also includes deep red, black, purple, and dark green. Suddenly, the possibilities are endless for creating very rich and deep paintings. Your life is the same. The only way to live a full, rich, and fulfilled life is to use all of who you are, the lighter parts and the darker parts, *in a balanced and controlled way*.

When you find this balance, free of denial and reactive behavior, you tap into your true power. In order to get to this point, you have to tread through your fear, anger, sorrow, desire, insecurities, and viewpoints.

The Practice of Developing the Respectful Self offers ways for you to start waking up again and to come out of numbness and remember what it feels like to be alive, content, energized, and empowered. You will experience yourself in a new way. This can be uncomfortable, maybe even frightening.

With Courageous Self-Reflection, you have the opportunity to reframe many viewpoints and unexamined assumptions that keep you from living the life you want to live. You also get the chance to take a journey of self-discovery to feel, in a real way, who you are in your true power. Then you can walk through the world as a peaceful member of society using your skills and wisdom to foster peace, respect, and cooperation.

THE POWER OF MOTIVATION
AND TAKING AN OATH

Since the process of learning a new discipline is arduous— filled with many challenges and distractions— setting a clear goal, knowing your motivation, and actually making an oath to follow through is essential.

———————————————————————————————————(?)

- *Why are you reading this book?*
- *What interests you about Respectful Confrontation?*
- *Is it for your personal fulfillment?*
- *Do you desire to have more of an impact in the world and success in what you do?*
- *Are you interested in improving your personal relationships?*
- *Are you ready to commit to influencing society on a larger scale?*

Lasting change can happen if each individual commits to being mindful of their own actions and finding ways to be a positive influence on others. When you choose to overcome your own reactive behavior and find creative ways to empower others, you will contribute to positive change in your relationships with your family, with your friends, at work, in your neighborhood, and in the larger community. Not only will you have a large impact on your surroundings, but you will also find inner peace, personal fulfillment, and a sense that your life has purpose and meaning.

This process starts with finding the proper motivation and committing to a goal. You tap into an enormous power when you take an oath and commit to a daily practice. It provides focus, direction, confidence, and conviction, and keeps you on track through tough and challenging times.

Many of us struggle to find ways to feel satisfaction and purpose. We flit from one teaching to another, searching for the one thing that will offer us inner peace and happiness. We allow our personal beliefs to be swayed by those with the loudest voices, without taking the time to see what we truly value. You get a glimpse into your deepest and highest self when you clarify for yourself what you hold dear and what is important to you.

_____ **(?)**

- *What are you willing to stand up for?*
- *What is most precious to you?*
- *What values resonate with you?*
- *What are you prepared to do to create more peace in your life and live with purpose, satisfaction, and confidence?*

Each one of us will respond differently to these questions. That is what makes us unique and ultimately holds the clues to what will bring us our deepest satisfaction.

Clarifying your values is an essential step in making life choices and tapping into your own innate wisdom and energy. When you make choices based on your personal values, you radiate confidence and peace and inspire others. Doubt, insecurity, and fear fall away and you attract success, achievement, and well-being.

The following exercise will help you establish what your true values are as well as clarify your own personal motivation for generating more peace, personal fulfillment, and cooperation in your life. It will also help you shed light on your motivation for reading this book, making the experience more substantial and beneficial.

- *Are you interested in Respectful Confrontation to improve yourself or your relationships with your friends, family, and community?*
- *Would you like to commit to the oath of the Respectful Confronter?*
- *Are you ready to engage with everyone you encounter in an openhearted way?*

It is important to be honest with yourself and base your decision on what you feel motivated to do in your heart as well as look at what you are capable of at this moment. Your oath can change after a time as you feel more confident to take on more responsibility. St. Francis of Assisi, thirteenth century Catholic friar and founder of the Franciscan Order said, "Start by doing what's necessary; then do what's possible; and suddenly you are doing the impossible." The choice to work on yourself and to take personal responsibility for your own behavior and actions makes an enormous contribution to shifting our society in a positive way.

CLARIFYING VALUES AND TAKING A PERSONAL OATH

**BEFORE YOU START THIS EXERCISE, REVIEW
"HOW TO USE THIS BOOK" ON PAGE 23**

PRELIMINARY STEPS

(see APPENDIX ONE on page 281 for details)

▷ **Choose a good time and location**

▷ **Start with the basic sitting pose**

▷ **Bring your attention to your center**

▷ **Place all of your attention on your breath**

MAIN STEPS

▸ **Get some paper or a journal and a pen**

If you enjoy drawing, you may want to get pens of different colors.

▸ **Take a look at the following list and read through each item**

Notice how each value makes you feel. Do you have any connection with the value? Did you feel some charge when you read it? Do you find that value important to you? Make notes.

VALUES

....

ACCOMPLISHMENT/SUCCESS	EQUALITY	LOYALTY
ACCOUNTABILITY	FAITH	MONEY
ACCURACY	FAMILY	PEACE/NON-VIOLENCE
BEAUTY	FREEDOM	PLEASURE
CALM	FRIENDSHIP	POWER
CHALLENGE	FUN	PROSPERITY/WEALTH
COLLABORATION	HARD WORK	SERVICE
COMMUNITY	INDEPENDENCE	SIMPLICITY
COMPETITION	INNOVATION	SKILL
CREATIVITY	JUSTICE	STATUS
DELIGHT IN BEING/JOY	KNOWLEDGE	TRADITION
DISCIPLINE	LEADERSHIP	TRUTH
EFFICIENCY	LOVE/ROMANCE	WISDOM

....

▸ **Choose ten values from the list**

After reading through this list, decide which of these values resonate with you the most. Which ones get you excited and energized?

Which ones are you willing to stand up for if you feel they are
being threatened or violated? Which ones inspire your creativity?
Write these ten values in your journal. Take your time before you
decide.

▸ **Choose five values from your list of ten**

Now we are getting deeper into the core of who you are. Of these
ten values, which would you say are your top five? Write these five
values in your journal. Take your time before you decide.

▸ **Choose three values from your list of five**

Of these five, which would you say are your three highest values? Write these three values in your journal. Once again, take your time before you decide.

Once you have your three top values, add them to the empty spaces in the statement below. Now read the statement to yourself a few times, either silently or out loud. Notice what you are feeling when you read it. Write your own statement if the wording I offer doesn't work for you.

....

"I realize that I have the fortunate circumstances in my life to ensure that I can bring purpose and meaning to my time here on this planet. I will find creative ways to bring about more personal fulfillment and harmony within myself, and empowerment to others, by tapping into my unique abilities and stemming from my core values of _____, _____ and _____."
I commit to living in a way that will create the most positive influence on myself and others, fostering peace, education, generosity, human rights, respect, a healthy environment, and equality for all citizens. I commit to practicing Respectful Confrontation in a skillful and creative way."

....

▸ **Write this statement in your journal or on a piece of paper**

Write it a number of times as a way to get familiar with it. Write it on a large piece of paper and hang it up where you can see it. You may want to memorize it.

▸ **Be silent, breathe, and focus on this oath**

Notice what happens when you contemplate your highest values —the core of who you are— and this personal oath. Notice the feelings that arise. Notice the energy that flows. Allow yourself to feel the power when you connect with your highest values, clear intention, and purpose.

CLOSING STEPS

(see APPENDIX ONE on page 283 for details)

▷ **Shake out and stretch your legs**

▷ **Make notes on what you have discovered**

 TIPS

There is no right or wrong way to do this exercise. Listen to your heart and aspects of yourself will be revealed. Making decisions in your life should be easy once you are clear about what you value most. All you need to do is ask if the choices you make align with your chosen values. What are you doing with your time, habits, career choices, and other aspects of your life? Look at the people you hang out with. Choosing to do things and be with people who align with your values will energize you and lead you to fulfillment and satisfaction.

This is your personal declaration and oath. When you find yourself getting distracted, doubting your own abilities or losing interest in this process and these practices, go back to your declaration and allow it to energize and inspire you to get back on track.

"I have always had great ideas and started new projects. But none of them ever went anywhere. I would try to connect with people, without success. Then I got centered and made it a point to stay present. I am now following through. And the funny thing is that people are noticing me more without me having to try!"

THE POWER OF PRESENCE AND CENTEREDNESS

Now that you have established a clear motivation, it's time to start doing some work on yourself. This starts with centering yourself and becoming present. When you choose to navigate the bumpy, inward path, as well as engage with others in an openhearted way, it is important to stay connected to yourself, to stay open to what is happening at that moment, and also find your way back to your core when you get distracted or thrown off.

Having your body in a particular place is one level of presence. For example, that's what I said in school when the teacher called my name:

"Joe?"

"Present."

But was I really present? My body may have been there. But where were my thoughts? Was I aware of the fly on the wall? Did I notice that I was hungry? That Sandra was trying to pass me a note? Or that I was happy or sad?

Being fully present and centered connects you to all of yourself—your physical body, emotions, sensations, and thoughts— and opens you to a strong awareness of where you are and what is happening around you.

When centered, you walk through life in a conscious way ready to take advantage of opportunities and mindfully avoid those things that are harmful or distracting. You easily assert yourself and also react quickly to any and all input that comes your way. All of your actions come from your core—leading to balance, flow, and integration. You are both strong and graceful.

You can see how this presence and centeredness is essential for succeeding in different areas of your life: in work, relationships, personal growth, and maintaining your health. People in high-stress jobs, like teachers and nurses, will have more ease and longevity in their career if they maintain a level of centeredness. This also applies to parents and students.

You see this in athletes, politicians, and prominent leaders from history, like the Dalai Lama and Martin Luther King, Jr. By remaining centered and fully present in all situations, they were able to overcome distractions and obstacles to achieving their goals.

THE CENTER, AWARENESS, AND DEEPER LISTENING

The center referred to in the Chinese disciplines as the "tan tien" and in the Japanese practices as the "hara", is located in the core of your body: about three finger-widths below the navel and about one-third of the way into the body from the front.

Even though your center is not a real organ in your body, it definitely has a presence. With many nerves that flow through this area and close to many of your vital organs, it a highly sensitive and active part of you.

This is your place of personal power, personal identity, awareness, creativity, and desire to connect, and where the impulse to take action originates. According to Taoist principles, your center is where you open to awareness and where you perceive things. The cultivation of "coming from your center" in all that you do is the foundation for success in many skills, like sports and dance, and is considered an important part of most martial arts and meditation practices.

When you have developed a strong connection to your center, you tap into your own personal power and creativity, following appropriate impulses with confidence and ease. By placing your attention in your center, you open to deeper levels of noticing and listening.

Noticing is one of the most valuable tools in self-development, healing, and how you relate to the world. When you are present and centered, you use a more sophisticated way of listening that includes your ears, your eyes, your whole body, your feelings, and your full experience. Your whole being comes alive. There is a much richer and more detailed world around you and you are a much more intricate being than you may think. All you need to do is take the time to notice. Noticing is also an important element in maintaining peaceful interaction with others. You can't resolve a problem or change a bad habit if you aren't first aware that it is there.

Deeper listening is an essential part of the practice of Respectful Confrontation. By listening in this way, you learn to pick up on subtle signals that go beyond what is heard or spoken. You have the ability to "hear with your heart" and navigate feelings, belief systems, anxiety, and fear. This allows you to make informed decisions that are supported by information that goes far beyond the spoken word or what is seen on the surface. This helps you to open to your innate wisdom and also gives you the confidence to take action from a place of conviction.

Have you ever made decisions that were based on a deeper knowing? Have you ever done something that others thought was odd but you knew that it was the right thing to do? Can you hear beyond what someone says and connect with something that is unspoken? This is the result of deeper listening.

What follows are two exercises that familiarize you with your center and help you develop more presence. The more you do these exercises, the quicker they will become healthy, empowering habits.

E X E R C I S E
GET CENTERED

**BEFORE YOU START THIS EXERCISE, REVIEW
"HOW TO USE THIS BOOK" ON PAGE 23**

PRELIMINARY STEPS

(see APPENDIX ONE on page 281 for details)

▷ **Choose a good time and location**

▷ **Start with the basic sitting pose or the basic standing pose**

MAIN STEPS

▸ **Focus on your center**

Focus on a spot three finger-widths below your navel, somewhere in the center of your lower belly. Try to see this point with your mind's eye. Notice any sensations and feelings while focusing on your center.

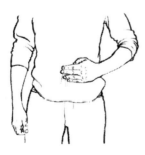

▸ **Make this point as tangible as possible**
Place your index finger in front of your navel. Place all four of your fingers next to each other, resting on your lower belly. Notice where your pinky finger rests and feel that point. From that point, bring your awareness inside your body about one-

third of the way from the front of your abdomen to the back. Keep your focus on this point.

If you are the type of person who works well with images, you may want to visualize an image at this point, like a flower, a ball or anything that will help you to keep connected to this point.

▸ **Breathe naturally from your center**

Listen to your natural breath and let your belly relax with each breath. Breathe out through your mouth. Notice your belly moving inward towards your spine. Breathe in slowly through your nose without creating any tension. Notice your belly expanding. Hold the breath for a moment and then simply release the breath. There is no need to push out the breath. Just let it pour out of your body. Breathe in fully and breathe out fully. Exert yourself on the inhalation, and practice fully letting go on the exhalation.

Continue to breathe into this area and notice if you feel any sensation. *Don't do anything with what you notice; just take note of how it feels. Let it flow.*

▸ **Notice when you stop focusing on your center**

Notice as quickly as possible when you get distracted—the quicker, the better. When you realize you are distracted, think of your center, and bring your attention back to it. Keep repeating this process until you come to the end of the exercise.

CLOSING STEPS

(see APPENDIX ONE on page 283 for details)

▷ **Shake out and stretch your legs.**

▷ **Make notes on what you have discovered.**

RECOMMENDED SCHEDULE

Start with ten to fifteen minutes. I recommend you do this exercise every day in the beginning. This exercise is the basis for all of the other exercises in this book. Mastering this will make it easier to practice the other exercises. In fact, it is a longer version of the Preliminary Steps for each exercise.

 TIPS

You can do this exercise either standing or sitting. I find it most effective to stand, but if it is difficult for you to stand for a long period of time, do it in a seated position. Or try switching off from one day to the next, standing and sitting, so you get a sense of the subtle differences and keep the exercise from getting tedious. Try doing this exercise while you are at work or with friends. Try staying engaged with others and still focus on your center.

There is no right way or wrong way to do this. Be aware of how you experience this exercise. The goal is to increase the amount of time you stay focused on your center and, more importantly, to shorten the amount of time you are distracted. Many of us can go hours before we realize we are not centered and present.

REMEMBER: *you are expected to get distracted; the success lies in how quickly you notice it!*

PRESENCE AND DEEPER LISTENING

**BEFORE YOU START THIS EXERCISE, REVIEW
"HOW TO USE THIS BOOK" ON PAGE 23**

PRELIMINARY STEPS

(see APPENDIX ONE on page 281 for details)

▷ **Choose a good time and location**

▷ **Start with the basic sitting pose**

▷ **Bring your attention to your center**

▷ **Place all of your attention on your breath**

MAIN STEPS

▸ **Become aware of yourself**

Start with your body. What kind of sensations do you feel? Then notice your emotions and then your thoughts. There's no need to do anything with this information. All you need to do is *notice*.

▸ **Become aware of your surroundings**

Start with your eyes closed. What do you hear? What do you feel? What do you sense? How do these things influence you? Now open your eyes. What do you see? Be as detailed as possible.

▸ **Name the things you notice**

Without judging, simply whisper or think the things that come into your awareness, both internally and externally. For instance: *There is tension in my leg. The wind is blowing the curtain. I can smell food cooking. I'm feeling a bit tired.* Do this until you come to the end of the exercise. Don't stop naming things; stay focused on what you notice.

CLOSING STEPS

(see APPENDIX ONE on page 283 for details)

▷ **Shake out and stretch your legs**

▷ **Make notes on what you have discovered**

RECOMMENDED SCHEDULE

Start with five minutes, at least three times a week. Add more time as you get more familiar with the process. When you begin to master this exercise, you will become more grounded and aware of what is going on around you.

 TIPS

One thing that gets in the way of opening to deeper levels of listening is judging the things you see, hear or feel. Judging is different from noticing. When you are listening in the proper way, your thoughts may be something like: *I hear a bird. I feel a breeze. I see a spot on the wall.* Keep those thoughts coming. Don't stop.

If your thoughts sound like this, then you are no longer in the present and noticing what is happening now: *That damn bird is making so much noise. I'm cold, why didn't I turn on the heat?*

Stupid me. Look at that spot on the wall. The people who live here are slobs. You are judging and throwing yourself into the past and future, and avoiding the present. This is what happens when you drop out of present awareness and into your scattered mind.

When your mind wanders, get back to listening to what is around you or within you. If you start to get discouraged, bored or distracted, don't judge yourself. Acknowledge that those things are part of the present moment and worth noticing.

This exercise helps you to stay engaged with the present moment and develop sensitivity to what is unfolding around you so you can quickly and wisely take action.

Although they may seem simple, these exercises have enormous power. If you can find five to ten minutes a day to do them, you will notice that your life will change. You will feel safer and more at home in the world, and you will feel less distracted and find that you can get things done in a quicker, more efficient way. You will have less tension, aches, and pains, and feel generally happier and lighter. You will learn to trust your intuition more and connect with others more easily.

"Redefining power has given me hope. I now see that my sensitivity and caring nature are actually powerful qualities; I don't have to be right all the time. I can yield in a powerful way and try to find solutions. The stronger I get with this practice, the more freedom I feel."

THE FOUR PILLARS OF TRUE POWER: **GROUNDING, FOCUS, STRENGTH** AND **FLEXIBILITY**

Another important element to developing the Respectful Self is to increase personal power. There is a direct connection with personal power and how you view yourself in the world, your level of comfort in engaging with others, and your ability to assert your truth. Personal power is also related to your self-confidence, how much of an impact you have on the world, and how much you are able to fulfill your life purpose and live out your true potential.

In order for you to open fully to your own potential and to other people, a distinction needs to be made between *true power* and *brute force*. Most of human history has been shaped by a false belief that power is limited to something outside of us. Human beings lived relatively peacefully as nomads from earliest times until about 10,000 BCE, when they started to cultivate crops, domesticate animals, and establish social classes. This is known as the Neolithic Revolution. This major turning point in human history, when humans began to live in civilizations, led to a need to protect property, ensure good crops, and obtain more land and goods to survive. Using brute force to obtain power and resources became commonplace.

Most wars and crime are motivated by a need to possess resources or guard something that seems precious. With this belief, the smartest thing to do would be to obtain as much power as possible, using any means possible, including murder, slavery, destroying the opponent, abusing earth's resources, war, and genocide. Mahatma Gandhi said, "The earth provides enough to satisfy every man's needs, but not every man's greed."

And in personal and professional relationships, we see the same dynamic played out with manipulation, gossip, deceit, financial scandals, and secrets.

Over time, we have developed a strong belief that the only one who succeeds is the one with the biggest weapon and the sooner we disempower our opponents the stronger we are. Sharing is not an option. Respecting and understanding those who are different is not an option. The means justify the ends, even if it means breaking laws.

The funny thing is that, *after thousands of years of choosing this world view, we have forgotten that it is simply one option to choose from.* This old-fashioned view of power is not what I would call *true power* but rather a strategy to use brute force to impose one's will and ensure one's success at the expense of others. George Washington, founding father and first president of the United States, said, "Arbitrary power is most easily established on the ruins of liberty abused by licentiousness."

By tapping into your true power, you discover that you are more vital and capable than you thought you were. You discover that your own personal power is unlimited and you overcome limited perceptions of yourself and the world around you. This leads to a renewed sense of confidence in yourself and others and the ability to respect, understand, and creatively collaborate with others.

The need to dominate, covet, hoard, and disempower falls away because you let go of the paranoid fear that you may lose power. How can you lose something when you know that it resides within you and is unlimited?

As a young boy, I didn't fit into the current definition of a powerful man, where brute force, destruction, and disrespectful competition for the sake of profit were rewarded. Because I wasn't the strongest and I cared about how others were feeling, I fell into the group of "nice guys" who were told that we would never know what it would be to be powerful.

Well, I wasn't satisfied with that! I felt like I was powerful in my own way. I felt like I had enormous energy and abilities to have a positive impact on the world. I felt like I could assert myself in a way that didn't harm others and didn't require me to have big biceps or become ruthless. I was determined to find a new definition of power that suited me and those like me. I was determined to not only redefine power for me and others like me, but to offer a new paradigm of personal power that would usher in an age of peace for the twenty-first century!

I have used all my encounters with cultures around the world and all my life experiences to examine what real power is. If true power is not just brute force, what is it? Yes, strength is an important aspect of power, but what else is involved? I looked to martial arts to find my answer. I thought about the different ways my teachers trained me to develop my technique and improve my form. I thought about the masters who, in their eighties, can still defeat opponents half their age or younger. How do they do it?

I concluded that to truly be in your power, *strength must be balanced with grounding, focus, and flexibility.* Although they are developed separately, they support and enhance each other. Strength is one of the Four Pillars of True Power, but it is not necessarily the most important.

To be in your true power, you must have an equal mastery of all four qualities. Without this, you will be out of balance and have challenges to accomplishing your goals. If even one of them is lacking or not stable, you will always be operating at a deficit. This pertains to all areas of your life. Think about athletes. Could a gymnast get top scores with physical strength alone? What does it take for someone to be a successful negotiator? Is bullying enough? How about a good teacher or parent? They all need an equal amount of the Four Pillars of True Power.

When you are secure in your grounding, focus, strength, and flexibility and you know you have reached a certain level of proficiency in these areas, you will walk through life with the confidence needed to achieve anything you choose. Having talents like physical strength or great focus are valuable assets on your path to fulfillment and reaching your goals, but they can only go so far. A person who has taken the time to truly develop a moderate level of all four pillars will, in the end, be stronger, more capable, and more likely to succeed than someone who is extraordinary in just one area.

By embracing these principles, you will discover that each of the four powers allows you to tap into a unique source of internal energy. Not only do these four qualities improve your performance and how you function in the world, they will help sustain you when you take on challenges and take risks, increasing your probability of success and personal fulfillment. Mastering the Four Pillars of True Power is essential when communicating with others, especially in challenging confrontations.

PILLAR ONE: **GROUNDING**

Let's start with the power of grounding. Like all things in life, building something requires starting with a strong foundation. When your foundation is strong, then you have the confidence to grow, take risks, build on your experiences, and reach for your highest potential.

All martial arts begin with establishing a relationship between you and the ground. Many beginning exercises help you to develop a strong sense of balance, a sense of sure footing, a comfort in falling and getting back up, an awareness of gravity, and the benefits of working within that force.

When a martial artist feels grounded, she is confident to do leaps, to kick, to take risks and "fly" because she knows she will always land with secure footing and find her stability. The more confidence she has in her grounding, the bigger the leaps she will take.

The dynamic of grounding is *downward-moving*. The lower body is engaged and we use this downward force to stay balanced, unwavering, and unmovable when necessary The element that is associated with grounding is *water*. If you observe rivers, you will see that they flow from higher to lower altitudes. All sources of water manage to find their way to lower ground.

Grounding provides a sense of connection with the earth and a feeling of being at home in the world. It leads to an unwavering self-confidence and conviction in what you do and believe. With a strong personal philosophy, you can't be easily swayed from your beliefs. It is hard to be manipulated when you know what you believe; you stand strong and always land on your feet when challenged.

Grounding helps you to find flow in your life and can even support you in harnessing gravity. Gravity is a powerful force. To go against gravity takes enormous amounts of energy reserves. You build up tension in the body by walking through life with a sense that you have to hold yourself up. Think about phrases that we tend to use: *Pull yourself up. Keep your chin up. Hold your head up high.* When you learn to yield to gravity, you let go of unnecessary holding and align with the natural flow of things around you.

The tendency to fight the force of gravity comes from the slow process of humans losing connection with the earth. When we were nomadic people, we understood the power of the earth and how much the earth supported us. We felt held and nurtured by the earth. This gave us confidence and a sense of feeling at home. As we became more urbanized after the Neolithic Revolution around 10,000 BCE, we lost our intimate contact with the earth, and subsequently, we lost our sense of belonging, security, and grounding.

Black Elk, a Native American spiritual leader and prominent figure in nineteenth century American history, illustrated the importance of our relationship with the earth when he said, "Hear me, four quarters of the world—a relative I am! Give me the strength to walk the soft earth, a relative to all that is! Give me the eyes to see and the strength to understand, that I may be like you. With your power only can I face the winds." Not relying on the earth's stable foundation takes a lot of energy. And we wonder why we are so tired.

When you develop your power of grounding, you let go of holding yourself up and feeling that you are alone. You stop working against the natural flow of things and have more energy to put into other things. Tapping into gravity and grounding gives you new reserves of internal and natural energy with which to work.

Master grounding and you will develop a stronger relationship with yourself, with your surroundings, and with others. You will develop a keen awareness that allows you to be more alert to the signals around you. This will assist you in fending off danger and confidently engaging in opportunities that lead to growth, success, and connection.

The more you are aware of your surroundings and know that you can take care of yourself, the less paranoid and nervous you will be. You will let go of your fear-based barriers that cause separation and keep people at a distance. You will replace hypervigilance with natural, relaxed awareness and walk through the world in a centered, confident way.

The following exercise, "Elephant Walking", is one of the first things I learned with my Tai Chi practice and also provides the basis for most martial arts. Simple to learn, it ensures sure footing, balance, and a foundation for all other powers, skills, and maneuvers. I make sure to incorporate this exercise in all of my workshops and seminars. It is effective, powerful, and fun to do.

Think about how elephants walk. For such large animals, they move with grace and confidence. They are methodical in their movement, and when they need to, they can move very quickly. They seem very grounded and connected to the earth. Lama Lhundrup, Abbot of Kopan Monastery, compared the elephant to the mind, saying, "An elephant walks steadily and cannot be stopped. He walks with confidence and certainty, and his mindfulness is completely balanced. With panoramic awareness he walks through the jungle; his senses are very keen. This open-minded interest, however, does not make him lose his inner balance. Mindfulness in tune with movement is what leads to liberation. It is a sure movement that cannot be stopped, full of dignity, not agitated, with a panoramic view, and it has a playful lightness and intelligence to it." This is a great description of the benefits of mastering the power of grounding.

The feet of an elephant are flat. When they walk, they step out with one foot, distributing their weight into the other three legs. They then place their forward-moving foot on the ground with no weight, making sure that where they step is safe, secure, and will support them. When they are sure they are on stable ground they shift weight into that foot, which propels them forward.

In order for us two-legged humans to move forward, we have to allow ourselves to fall. Try it. Go and walk for a few minutes and notice that what you are actually doing is falling and catching yourself with every step you take. This requires an enormous amount of work for your body and more specifically your pelvis.

"Elephant Walking" helps to alleviate the stress of falling into your steps, which might reduce lower back pain. You move gracefully, shift speeds with skill, change directions with ease, and maintain a strong sense of balance and stability. As you get more familiar with this exercise, you will also notice that your feet become like your eyes. You develop a heightened awareness of your surroundings and what feels stable to you because you use your feet to "feel out" what's around you.

So let's try it.

EXERCISE

ELEPHANT WALKING

**BEFORE YOU START THIS EXERCISE, REVIEW
"HOW TO USE THIS BOOK" ON PAGE 23**

PRELIMINARY STEPS

(see APPENDIX ONE on page 281 for details)

▷ **Choose a good time and location**

▷ **Start with the basic standing pose**

▷ **Bring your attention to your center**

▷ **Place all of your attention on your breath**

MAIN STEPS

▶ **Place foot. Take your first step with no weight in the foot**

Keep your legs bent. Start with one foot and step out in front of you, not too far from you. Keep all your weight on your back leg and place this foot on the ground with no weight. It is important to place your whole foot at once on the floor, not toe first or heel first.

▶ **Shift weight into the foot**

Once you have placed the foot flat on the floor without putting any weight into it, shift the weight from the back leg to the front leg.

▶ **Place second foot, no weight in foot**

Then lift the second leg, keeping your knees slightly bent and place it out in front of you, flat on the floor and with no weight. Once the foot has fully touched the ground, shift your weight into that foot.

▶ **Walk forward for one to five minutes**

You may want to whisper to yourself: *place foot, shift weight, place foot, shift weight.* Keep your knees slightly bent. Take small steps. This, of course, will seem an odd way to walk, but keep practicing it. When you walk this way you will notice that you always have balance and connection with the ground. Continue breathing in a deep and steady way.

▶ **Walk sideways for one to five minutes**

When you have done a few minutes of walking forward, now do the same thing walking sideways. You don't need to look. Trust that by placing your foot without weight first to feel out where you are going will give you all the information you need to ensure you are not going to fall or step on something or someone. Don't think about it; let your body figure it out. Trust your feeling. Trust your awareness.

▸ **Walk backwards for one to five minutes**

Now try walking backwards. Go slow! And remember to keep your knees bent. There is no need to look behind you if you go slowly, keep your knees bent, and first place the foot without weight. This will seem very strange, even scary, if you have never done this before. Take your time. Most martial artists will train for years before they develop a strong sense of grounding and heightened awareness. If you feel that walking backwards is too much for you, practice walking forward until you feel confident with this new technique.

▸ **Walk in all three directions until you end the exercise**

Have fun exploring different rhythms, moving in all directions, without looking.

CLOSING STEPS

(see APPENDIX ONE on page 283 for details)

▷ **Shake out and stretch your legs**
▷ **Make notes on what you have discovered**

RECOMMENDED SCHEDULE

Doing this exercise a few times can help you understand the power of grounding. *If you do this exercise regularly, you will develop a stronger connection with the earth, stability, and a keen sense of awareness.* I recommend you do it at least three times a week for at least fifteen minutes, walking in all directions. It may get tedious, but the repetition will help you understand the deeper powers that lie within grounding.

TIPS

If you get tired, take a break and shake out your legs. After you do the exercise for a while, you can increase your speed and amount of time. But remember, no matter how fast you go you must always have the awareness that you are placing your foot without weight first before you shift it.

OVERVIEW OF GROUNDING

DYNAMIC
Downward-moving

ELEMENT
Water

CORRESPONDING PRACTICE
The Practice of Developing the Respectful Self

BENEFITS
Sensitivity, keen awareness, clear personal philosophy
and value system, unwavering conviction, anchored, confident,
free of doubt, stable, intuitive

WAYS TO DEVELOP GROUNDING
"Elephant Walking", martial arts like Tai Chi (*I recommend The School of Tai Chi Chuan*) and Chi Kung (*I recommend The School of Tian Gong*), gardening, physical exercise, warm baths, rubbing feet on ground, wholesome foods, stillness, listening practice, being in nature, conscious touch (massage yourself or ask someone to massage you), clarifying values and personal philosophy, ritual and repetitive practice

PILLAR TWO: **FOCUS**

Now that you have started the process of grounding, you will notice that you are more aware of what is happening around you. You will be more sensitive to impressions, feelings, opportunities, energy, power, creativity, the actions of others, and your surroundings. You'll notice all the sensations in your body, all the emotions flowing through you, and all the thousands of thoughts running through your mind at any given moment. You will feel how vibrant and inspiring life can be.

However, that's a lot to take in. What do you do with all this? Having so many options can cause you to freeze, get distracted, and not take action. This is where focus comes in.

The innate force within focus manifests in two ways. The first is to find the stillness amongst the chaos; the second is to give direction to one's efforts. *The role of focus is to unify and stabilize all the impressions, creative energy, and experiences of life, and subsequently create a channel for this to flow in a constructive, intentional way.* This leads to success in communication, as well as realizing life goals.

The dynamic of focus has two directions. First, it has an *inward movement*, bringing you inside yourself to gather your own personal resources and channel your energies. Secondly, that inner focus is then taken *upward and outward* to reach desired goals with clarity and precision.

The element that is associated with focus is *fire*. Fire brings clarity to those things that are unclear, sluggish, and "wishy-washy". When you look at fire, it has the ability to hold your attention (inward focus). At the same time the force within the fire moves upwards through the flames and the smoke.

The wisdom of focus understands that life is never static; it never stands still. The most successful way to navigate through life is to have a clear idea of where you are now (inward focus), establish a clear picture of where you want to go, and then consciously plot the course of least resistance to get there (upward, outward focus). It is not the force of focus that actually gets you there. The power of strength—discussed in the next section—propels you forward. But in order to get somewhere, all the force in the world won't lead to success if you don't start with mental stability, precision, and a clear idea of where you are headed.

Think of the image of a boat out at sea. You may notice that your mind is like a stormy sea of emotions, thoughts, fears, doubts, and insecurities. Or you may notice that somewhere on your journey you get thrown off course and distracted. The inward force of focus first calms the waves of your mind to ensure smooth sailing. Then the upward, outward force of focus provides you with the rudder and sails on your boat, as well as a compass, and all the navigational tools and equipment you need, to plot a clear course towards your goal. This gets you to your destination in a quicker, more efficient way. Even if you get distracted for a moment, you know exactly how to get back on course.

When you tap into the power of focus, *you use less energy to reach your goal and you develop the skill of mindfulness.* You become aware of the state of your mind, you have certainty about your life direction, you approach things with precision and lightness, and you communicate in a way that is intentional. When you develop focus, you become more mindful of the impact of your thoughts, words, and actions and have the ability to choose when and how you will act and react to things.

When the mind is unfocused, we say things we don't mean, have emotional outbursts we can't stop until it's too late, and do things that we know are not good for us yet we do them anyway. Let's not forget about the thousands of needless, negative thoughts we think that tire us out and demotivate us.

The power of focus is essential for someone who practices Respectful Confrontation. Harm and conflict can only surface when we are mindlessly reactive or not conscious of the thoughts, feelings, and impulses that are arising. The Buddha said, "Whatever an enemy might do to an enemy, or a foe to a foe, the ill-directed mind can do to you even worse." Just think about how much of an influence you have on your surroundings, on the people around you, and on yourself. Have you noticed how you, or a family member or work colleague, can quickly affect the overall mood with words or even with facial expressions? Someone who has mastered the power of focus chooses to be responsible in creating a better world by staying mindful and lessening their reactive, harmful behavior.

Mastering focus in your communication is also an important tool in business settings. In a study from the University of Maryland's Robert H. Smith School of Business, researchers put a price tag on the cost of poor communication in American hospitals at $12 billion per year. We are vague, we waste energy to push to our goal, and we often have to repeat things before we finally get them done. When we clear our mind, focus on the desired target, and channel our energy, we don't need so much effort and our first attempt has the necessary impact. Energy saved! Efficient results!

While others are running around aimlessly, distracted by the slightest thing, overcome by emotional stress, arguing, and burning out, you walk through the world with calm, ease, determination, harmony with others and your surroundings, and see the slow, steady realization of your goals.

Here is an exercise to help you develop more focus, clarity, and the precision to channel your energy. After doing this a couple of times, you will understand how the power of focus can benefit you. If you choose to do this on a regular basis, you will develop new constructive habits that lead to mindfulness, achieving your goals, and better communication.

EXERCISE
"HEY" EXERCISE

**BEFORE YOU START THIS EXERCISE, REVIEW
"HOW TO USE THIS BOOK" ON PAGE 23**

PRELIMINARY STEPS

(see APPENDIX ONE on page 281 for details)

▷ **Choose a good time and location**

▷ **Start with the basic standing pose**

▷ **Bring your attention to your center**

▷ **Place all of your attention on your breath**

MAIN STEPS

▸ **Choose a point across the room**

This point could be something on a wall, a spot on a curtain or a branch of a tree. It should be far enough away and about the height of your eyes. Make that point small. Keep focusing on that point, like it's the center of a dart board.

▸ **Pretend to hit it with your force**

Breathe in deeply, and as you exhale, make a movement with one of your hands as if you are trying to hit that point with your force. This movement looks similar to throwing a dart or a ball.

X

▸ **Keep repeating the movement**

As you do it, check in to see how you are doing. Are you grounded, connected to the earth, bending your knees, and is the movement coming from your center?

▸ **Make adjustments – Force**

Do you have a feeling that you are hitting your target? If you were throwing a dart, would you hit the center of the board? First, check to see if you maintain the proper amount of force. Try giving it too much force and notice how that feels. A waste of your energy, right? Try giving it too little energy and notice that you miss your target; it falls short of your goal.

▸ **Make adjustments – Precision**

Now that you have the right amount of force, be sure to use the proper focus to hit that point. Not next to it, above it, or below it—the right amount of precision to hit it.

▸ **Use your voice with the word "Hey"**

When this motion begins to feel comfortable, add the word "Hey!" when you try to hit your mark, as if you are now talking to this point with your full intention and conviction. Keep repeating until you feel that you are using the same force in your voice as you are using in the movement. Repeat this for a few minutes until you end the exercise.

CLOSING STEPS

(see APPENDIX ONE on page 283 for details)

▷ **Shake out and stretch your legs**

▷ **Make notes on what you have discovered**

RECOMMENDED SCHEDULE

Start with five minutes to fifteen minutes, at least three times a week. When you get familiar with the power of this exercise, you will only need to do it for one minute to feel its benefits.

By doing this exercise a couple of times, you can really feel in your body how focusing on your target and determining the right amount of force can actually energize you. If you do this regularly, you will feel a flow of renewed energy moving through you. You will feel lighter, clearer, and more vital. You will communicate with clarity and be more effective in all that you undertake.

 TIPS

This may seem awkward at first. It is hard for many of us to use our voices in such a forceful way, but try it. If you are uncomfortable speaking with a loud voice, make sure no one is around to hear you. Start softly and see if you can bring more energy into your voice. The goal is to match the force in your voice with the force of your movement and get your voice to travel that full distance. So let it out! By channeling and focusing your force, you will discover the innate power in focus, as well as feel the power in your voice. This can be very healing. Notice how it feels to express in that way; notice how you sound. Don't judge; be curious. Enjoy.

As you do this, make sure you are inhaling and exhaling. Exhale as you "throw" the force.

OVERVIEW OF FOCUS

DYNAMIC
Inward and upward-moving

ELEMENT
Fire

CORRESPONDING PRACTICE
The Practice of Respectful Engagement

BENEFITS
Mindfulness, clarity, precision, clear vision, conservation of energy, efficiency in communication and time management, success in attaining goals, perseverance, clear direction and intention, healthy analysis, discrimination

WAYS TO DEVELOP FOCUS
"'Hey' Exercise", meditation, puzzles and word games, archery, darts, journaling, physical exercise like running, memorization, star-gazing, labyrinth walking, drawing, learning a musical instrument

PILLAR THREE: **STRENGTH**

Developing the powers of grounding and focus gives you a strong foundation to start with. You have mastered within yourself stability and efficiency. However, it is the power of strength that propels you forward. Like a young bird in its nest, you are now fully capable of sustaining yourself and ready to take flight. With a renewed sense of self, characterized by confidence, awareness, stability, calm, centeredness, clarity, and presence, it is now time to interact with others and realize your goals.

The power of strength takes you out of stasis and brings you into movement, adventure, and exploration. The dynamic of strength is *forward-moving*, and the element that is associated with strength is *earth*. Like rocks and the denser parts of the earth, your body is the densest part of who you are when you take into account your emotional, mental, and even spiritual aspects. The better you can make use of your body, and the more you can open to your courage, the more you will tap into powers that will help you manifest your goals and finish what you start. You will feel more confident about taking care of yourself and find it easier to engage with others.

The innate force within strength is expressed in two ways. The first is the *courage* to move out of your safe space and into the unknown, and the second is the *physical force* needed to accomplish your goals.

The power of strength offers you the courage to take risks, the courage to speak your truth, and to hear the truth of others. To be held accountable and to assert yourself in ways that are productive and welcoming are the true aspects of strength that lead to strong character and an increase of success in all endeavors. *Keeping your promises and asking for help are important parts of building lasting relationships and require the power of strength.*

The pillar of strength comes the closest to the old view of what power is—physical, brute force. There are, of course, benefits to a strong body and physical mastery. This is certainly a necessary aspect of true power. But it is not the only aspect; it is just one of four.

In our modern, urban age of remote controls, "drive-thru" services, and the Internet, taking care of your body by working out, eating well, and finding ways to develop physical endurance is essential. Actually you could say that *because* of the sedentary lifestyle that you have grown accustomed to, you must put effort into strengthening the body.

Looking back through history, our bodies were built to take on hard physical labor—first as nomadic people, then as hunters, then as farmers. Our bodies were constantly being used to their daily limits. And like cars, we need to maintain these amazing human machines that nature has constructed. When you leave your car sitting too long in the garage without use, or if you abuse the car, eventually the car won't function at its best. This is what happens to many people in urban areas where we tend to abuse our bodies or we don't keep them in shape. The news is filled with reports of the global increases in obesity, as well as the number of ailments due to stress and anxiety. Researchers predict that global pharmaceutical sales are expected to reach $1.1 trillion in the next ten years. It is essential that you keep your "machine" well-oiled, maintained, and used often to keep it at its peak performance.

When you let go of brute force and *mindfully* use the true power of strength to manifest your goals, open to your courage, and maintain good physical health, you avoid the destructive factors that have caused so much harm in the past. When strength is balanced with grounding, focus, and flexibility, there is no need to fear your own power; you embrace the forward-moving force that throws you out of balance and into the dance of life.

OVERVIEW OF STRENGTH

....

DYNAMIC

Forward-moving

ELEMENT

Earth

CORRESPONDING PRACTICE

The Practice of Respectful Offense

BENEFITS

Courage, physical strength, assertiveness, confidence,
comfort with taking risks, stamina, accountability

WAYS TO DEVELOP STRENGTH

Physical exercise, weight training, martial arts like Tae Kwan Do
(*I recommend The School of Black Bear Tae Kwan Do*) and Poekoelan
(*I recommend The School of Poekoelan Tjimindie Tulen*), balanced diet,
playing team sports, mountain climbing, practice speaking your truth,
practice hearing another's truth without getting defensive,
follow through with your commitments and agreements, seeking out
mentors/asking for help, public speaking/performance

....

MASTERING RESPECTFUL CONFRONTATION

PILLAR FOUR: **FLEXIBILITY**

So far you have developed a strong sense of awareness, you've learned to channel your forces, and you have committed to moving forward to manifest your dreams and connect with others. However, with all this powerful force asserting itself without stopping or yielding, you will create conflict and waste a lot of energy pushing against things that aren't going your way. Why? Because you haven't brought in the powerful force of flexibility.

There is an ancient Taoist story where the master asks the student, "Which is stronger, a mighty oak tree or a blade of grass?" The conclusion of a long discussion is "that in a heavy monsoon, the mighty oak will snap like a twig, but the blade of glass will always persevere." The Taoist master, Lao Tzu said, "A tree that is unbending is easily broken." In some situations, the strength of an oak tree is needed, and in other situations, the flexibility of a blade of grass is stronger. It is your task to develop both kinds of power and then have the wisdom to know which of the two to implement.

The element that is associated with focus is *air*. Air may not seem very substantial compared to earth or the other elements. You can't seem to get a hold of it. Yet, within air is oxygen, the most essential element necessary for survival on this planet. Also, air has the power to keep an airplane in the sky or blow down houses in a storm. Like the force of air, the power of flexibility is not to be underestimated! Like the Ninja masters who prided themselves on seeming invisible to their opponents, giving them a tremendous strategical advantage when they attacked, the fact that both air and flexibility are so hard to grasp is their strength.

Of the four pillars, flexibility may be the most illusive and challenging.

However, I believe it is the most powerful of the four and the one that takes you to your highest power. The potent force of flexibility will lead you to the next level of your evolution. The doorway to understanding, compassion and love, it is the only force that can eventually overcome brute force. American poet and leader of the Transcendentalist Movement, Ralph Waldo Emerson, said, "Before we acquire great power we must acquire wisdom to use it well."

While the dynamic of strength is forward-moving, the dynamic of flexibility is *backward-moving*. Again, this is not to be underestimated. Making the empowered choice to move backward does not mean you are weak or defeated. Standing your ground and still choosing to yield requires tremendous courage, strength, and skill.

The force of flexibility results in swiftness, agility, receptivity, cunning, wisdom, and "street smarts." Those who have mastered flexibility have the ability to stretch and bend, to twist and turn, to match any attack, and to overcome any obstacle. *You master the use of the skillful means to adapt and positively influence all situations with ease and conservation of energy.*

Flexibility allows you to yield to, and cooperate with, a constantly changing world. If you look at nature and all things in it, you will notice that the only way to ensure the survival of a species is if that species is able to adapt to its environment. If a species decides to stay still, not move or change, not seek support, alliance or cooperation, or develop new ways to persevere, it will die out. Or, it will cause the destruction of a lot of others in order to maintain the status quo. As long as we hold on to an idea that adapting is weak, things will never change.

When you use the power of flexibility, you use the wisdom to know that you are not always right, that your way isn't always the best way, and that true collaboration means that the end result is partially your contribution and partially that of others. You learn to utilize the circumstances presented to you to move you forward and you don't have to use as much energy to get things accomplished because there is no need to push against obstacles.

In fact, in the process of adapting and yielding to what is presented to you, you grow and get stronger. With every encounter, you are asked to use certain skillful means unique to that situation. If you are in familiar surroundings, you have an "arsenal" of ways to make that situation work for you. Each time you find yourself in a new situation, you have to use your creativity and power to increase your skill set; it's like you are upgrading your own internal "software". The larger your skill set, the wiser you become, and the more your true power is revealed.

Not only that, but if you move through life in a flexible way and adapt to others and what is around you, you will live longer, age more gracefully, lower your chance of stress-related illnesses, and feel free and light.

OVERVIEW OF FLEXIBILITY

....

DYNAMIC
Backward-moving, receptive

ELEMENT
Air

CORRESPONDING PRACTICE
The Practice of Respectful Defense

BENEFITS
Skillful means, resilience, creativity, spontaneity, patience, flow, lightness and less stress, openness to possibility, curiosity, wisdom, security, adaptability, enjoyable to be around, receptivity, stealth, collaborative attitude, diplomacy, "street smarts"

WAYS TO DEVELOP FLEXIBILITY
Stretching, yoga, martial arts like Aikido, dancing, camping, breath work, rest and relaxation, practice receiving, volunteering at schools or work with children, driving your car and yielding to everyone, visiting and studying foreign cultures

....

Although all **FOUR PILLARS OF TRUE POWER**

are needed in all four segments of Respectful Confrontation,

each one corresponds more specifically

to one of the segments:

....

GROUNDING

provides the foundation for

The Practice of Developing the Respectful Self

FOCUS

relates more to **The Practice of Respectful Engagement**

and is directly involved with the process of communication

STRENGTH

supports **The Practice of Respectful Offense**

FLEXIBILITY

enhances **The Practice of Respectful Defense**

UNDERSTANDING THE MASCULINE AND FEMININE PRINCIPLES

According to Taoist teachings, Yang, the forward-moving principle, characterized as being masculine, and Yin, the backward-moving, receptive, feminine principle, are the two forces that keep the universe in motion. This doesn't mean male and female, it is simply a way to describe them. Of course, men move backward and women move forward. When you assert the masculine principle, you are engaging the power of strength; when you use the feminine principle, you are tapping into the power of flexibility.

All things that exist in our universe are in a constant backward and forward dance with themselves and with all other things. Nothing in our universe stands still; nothing is concrete and unchanging. Try to find something that never dies, transforms or ages, or shifts from one form to another. The very nature of our universe is that it is in constant motion. We may think that we can stand still and be motionless, but at that same moment, our planet is speeding around the sun at a speed of 66,000 miles per hour, or 107,000 kilometers per hour!

In order to interact with the world, you must pull yourself out of stillness, balance, and comfort, and initiate within yourself the forward-moving masculine principle. This is, of course, on one level, very powerful. But, when you think about it, you have just thrown yourself into imbalance, making yourself weaker.

Let's look at an example from martial arts to illustrate this dynamic. Imagine throwing a punch or you could stand up and actually try it yourself. (Please note, even though I am using the example of a punch, I am not advocating hitting people as a way to engage!)

Let's imagine the punch in slow motion. You are standing, looking at the goal you want to punch about one yard (one meter) in front of you about the height of your chest. Before you throw a punch, you start from balance and *grounding*, and then you *focus* on your target. You make a fist and start moving that fist to the point you want to hit. Keep your feet on the ground. Remember, we are doing this in slow motion. Once you reach your target, stay there a moment.

What do you notice? What you may see is that a large portion of your weight is now out in front of you and that your back foot has slightly lifted off the ground. You will feel out of balance and no longer grounded. If that is the case, you are experiencing exactly what happens when you throw a punch. You may be exerting a lot of power, you may be asserting yourself, and you are activating your masculine principle, but at the same time you are putting yourself out of balance and making yourself an easy target!

Think about it. When you initiate the masculine principle, when you assert yourself, you are at your weakest. How about that for a shift in paradigms? This could change our views of offense and of the obsession to conquer and dominate. History shows us over and over again that leaders, empires, and nations that have carelessly exerted their masculine principle have ultimately toppled. Why? Because the obsession to keep pressing on and moving forward had depleted their power and resources and left them weak and open to attack.

Think of the great emperors like Alexander and Napoleon. They were very grounded, focused, and assertive. Despite advice from many, Alexander exhausted his armies and resources in his pursuit to reach the "ends of the world and the Great Outer Sea" ending with his defeat in India. Napoleon's thirst for power resulted in him launching an over-reaching battle resulting in his "Waterloo". What is missing is the wisdom to know when to adapt and yield, or stop and retreat.

This illustration emphasizes how important it is to *use the masculine principle wisely*. Nothing will happen in your life if you don't assert yourself. But it is valuable to understand that if you stay in the forward-moving principle, you are *always off-balance, and that is not healthy*. Think about your lifestyle. Most likely, much of your work and social life is spent in excessive outward and forward motion, causing stress and anxiety.

We were told to work hard, succeed financially, do it alone, be the best, win even at the expense of others, put work before relationship, and use unscrupulous competition. These are the philosophies and ways of a society out of balance in its masculine principle. We develop stress-related illnesses, can't seem to connect with others, and we feel unfulfilled. This goes for both men and women!

The first step to moving towards a society based on cooperation and respect is to acknowledge that we all are living in this out-of-balance way and are all responsible for the present situation. By first recognizing that this extreme use of the masculine principle leads to destruction and then admitting that we *all* have had moments where we acted in this way, we can begin to heal the centuries-old pains and wounds of mindless, destructive masculine power from which we *all* suffer—both men and women. This doesn't mean that the masculine principle is bad. Not at all. *The masculine principle is only destructive when it is used unconsciously and irresponsibly.* Classical Greek philosopher Plato said, "The measure of a man is what he does with power."

The masculine principle is essential for growth, creativity, and for relationships to begin and develop. Without it, we all stagnate and we atrophy. A flower would never be pollinated if a bee didn't get into its masculine principle and go out seeking nourishment. A Mona Lisa would never have been painted if an artist hadn't grabbed some paint and a canvas and had the confidence and perseverance to create a masterpiece.

To be assertive requires humility and reverence. To step out of what is safe and familiar, not knowing what the consequences might be, demands courage and unwavering confidence.

However, once you get moving and throw yourself out of balance, it is essential to follow with the feminine principle and move back into balance. When you can live in alignment with this force of shifting naturally between the masculine and feminine principles, you find contentment, fulfillment, and harmony with all things. When you feel in harmony with all things, the chances of getting into an argument or creating conflict are slim, and your interactions remain beneficial, collaborative, and peaceful.

Let's take a look at that punch again. When you throw your punch, you have just asserted yourself and hopefully had the effect you wanted to have on your opponent.

As we have already established, you are now off balance and open to attack. You are at your weakest. To get back your power, step back into your center again, and get back into balance. Now that you are back in your balance and power, you are at an advantage to anticipate the next attack of your opponent. When it comes, you quickly assess what is coming, use your flexibility to get out of the way, and choose the most effective counter-move to take advantage of the fact that your opponent is now off balance and an easy target.

By using the receptive force in the feminine principle, you turn your opponent's attack to your advantage *by turning the energy of his attack back onto him, to throw him off, and defeat him.* Unlike cowering in defeat or running away, this approach makes receptivity and defending yourself a powerful strategy and necessary tool.

Many may think that a backward-moving, receptive action is passive. Not at all. Passivity and weakness are ways to run away from life. The feminine principle requires the courage and self-confidence to stand your ground in the face of adversity and use whatever comes your way to persevere and succeed; this brings you in contact with your true power.

Your power of strength, the masculine principle, gets you moving. Your power of flexibility, the feminine principle, is how you come back to your true self. By trusting that everything that is out of balance finds its way back to center, you begin to get a glimpse into the mysteries of the universe and the very things that make life happen. When you have the courage and centeredness to use the backward-moving, receptive principle, you truly open to the present moment and to all that life has to offer.

Ultimately, when you integrate the two and understand the dance of assertion and receiving, you have an open engagement with others, with your surroundings, and with yourself. You shed parts of yourself that could be considered weak, you open to your vulnerability, and you feel the tremendous force of life freely flowing through you. It is from your vulnerability that your true power is revealed.

ASSESSING YOUR FOUR PILLARS OF TRUE POWER

As you can see, reframing power in this way has deep ramifications for creating a world built on respect and mutual empowerment. Each of the Four Pillars of True Power provides an important set of skills and each one ignites an innate source of power that is lying dormant when these qualities are not consciously cultivated. As you tap into these powers, you live your life with a sense of security, ease, and generosity.

When you feel secure in yourself, you are more likely to encourage others to claim their own true power. You naturally feel the urge to be of service to others, creating a world where cooperation and respect become the norm, instead of conquering, disempowering, and coveting. With understanding and forgiveness instead of anger, fear, and revenge, you see competition as a fun, exciting way to help your opponents grow and strive for their own "personal best". These are the ways of true power.

This formula won't work if you only develop one or two of the four pillars. This would leave you out of balance. An excess of any one of these four can work against you, can be harmful to you and to others, and may even sabotage your attempts for personal fulfillment and the manifestation of your dreams.

For instance, people who have a strong mastery of grounding, but not focus, strength or flexibility, may be very sensitive, very aware of their surroundings, and strong in their beliefs, but they don't seem to be able to budge on their viewpoints. They never seem to grow and the subtle signals and energies they pick up from others distract them. Leaning towards paranoia, they may lose all their friends and may literally never leave the house.

Those who have developed focus, but not grounding, strength or flexibility, may become too narrow-minded in their approach to life and their dealings with others. They tend to obsess on details and, like a mouse that finds itself in the dead-end of a maze, get trapped in their own mind games. They can be incredibly judgmental, self-conscious, hypercritical of themselves and others, and fear to take any risks.

People who master strength, not grounding, focus or flexibility, push their way into things, bully others, and create chaos and dissension wherever they go. They may get things accomplished, but they probably don't have any trusted relationships. They may have a lot of enemies, and if people form alliances with them, it will probably be out of fear. Living by the edict "might is right" and not really concerned with justice, they never rest and find peace. These are the ones among us who usually get heart attacks at an early age.

Those who have a strong mastery of flexibility, not grounding, focus or strength, never seem to get anything done. They end up following the crowd, hoping that the crowd will choose to do something they would like to do. If not, they grin and bear it. They tend to remain unnoticed, finding it safe to stay at home and watch TV or spend hours with computer games. They try to keep everyone else happy and peaceful, avoiding all arguments or confrontations. This usually implies that they sacrifice their own needs and desires for the sake of "keeping the peace".

Get the picture? These are just a few examples of many permutations of what it looks like when the four pillars are out of balance. *A truly powerful person is someone who has equally developed all four pillars of grounding, focus, strength, and flexibility.* Think of the legs of a table. It doesn't matter how long the legs are, as long as the four legs are the same length; otherwise the table will tip and teeter. The same is true for people. We become truly powerful in body, mind, heart, and spirit when we have developed an equal level of skill in grounding, focus, strength, and flexibility. Someone with a moderate yet equal development of all four of these qualities is ultimately more powerful than someone who is only physically strong.

The following exercise is a useful tool to help you evaluate how you have cultivated up until this moment each of the Four Pillars of True Power in your life. If you are like most people, you probably don't have an equal mastery of the four pillars. By taking an honest look at where you are in your own personal development, you will have a clear picture of how to improve your skills and move toward an equal mastery. All paths to personal growth start with an accurate assessment of where you currently are.

How focused are you? How grounded? How strong and how flexible? You can apply this to your life in general, or you can take different aspects of your life, like your work life or your relationships, and do a separate assessment of each. I would start with one general assessment. Practice Courageous Self-Reflection and radical honesty. There is no need to fool yourself into thinking you are more proficient in an area. There is no need to judge yourself as good or bad for what you have or haven't developed.

EXERCISE

SELF PORTRAIT OF TRUE POWER

**BEFORE YOU START THIS EXERCISE, REVIEW
"HOW TO USE THIS BOOK" ON PAGE 23**

PRELIMINARY STEPS

(see APPENDIX ONE on page 281 for details)

▷ **Choose a good time and location**

▷ **Start with the basic sitting pose**

▷ **Bring your attention to your center**

▷ **Place all of your attention on your breath**

MAIN STEPS

▸ **Get some paper or a journal and a pen**

If you enjoy drawing, you may want to get pens of different colors.

▸ **Contemplate each power of the Four Pillars of True Power (Grounding, Focus, Strength, and Flexibility) one at a time.**

Think about the gifts, benefits, and innate power of each pillar.

(Review this chapter for an explanation of each of the four pillars) How well have you developed each? Don't think of them as theories; make them personal. How do they fit into your life? What is your relationship with each one? Which ones seem very familiar to you? Which ones trigger fear? Do you have a clear personal philosophy (grounding)? Do you follow through on commitments (focus)? Are you comfortable asserting yourself (strength)? Are you a good listener (flexibility)? These are just a few of many possibilities. You may want to ask friends what they think of you as a way to get a more accurate assessment.

► **Make notes on what you have discovered**

What are your strengths and challenges with each pillar? Find a way to compare your mastery of each one. You might do it with percentages or with a graph. You may do it with key words.

► **Draw yourself as a table**

After you have studied your notes, take a clean piece of paper and draw a tabletop. Your tabletop can look any way you want it to. Now, draw the four legs of your table, each leg representing one of the four pillars of true power. *Draw the legs in a way that illustrates how developed each pillar of power is in your life.* For instance, you may feel you are very adept at focusing, so your focus leg could be as thick as a tree; you may feel you are totally inflexible, so your flexibility leg might look like a toothpick next to your focus leg.

Be creative with what your tabletop and its legs look like. Have fun with it. The point of the drawing is for you to see in one clear image what kind of table you have.

► **Label each of the corresponding legs of your table: Grounding, Focus, Strength and Flexibility.**

Here is an example:

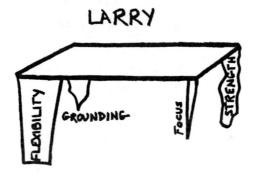

▸ **Take a look at your table**

This is a self-portrait of you. This is what you look like in relationship to true power. Notice what feelings come up. Notice what insights you get. Did you learn something new about yourself?

▸ **Assess your current situation**

What does your table look like? Is it stable? Wobbly? If you are like me, you will see that your legs have different lengths. It is unstable and not capable of fulfilling its purpose which is to be a balanced table to put things on.

Now take a look at your own life. If your table legs are uneven, then you are not functioning at your optimum level. The ultimate goal of this practice is to get the legs of your table to be of equal length. Your self-portrait is like a road map that gives you a clear inventory of what your next steps need to be.

▸ **Create a plan of action**

By consciously developing the four pillars, you will tap into your true power. Create a program for yourself to develop an equal mastery of all four powers. Review the suggested exercises listed in the overview for each of the Four Pillars of True Power, or choose other practices you can think of to increase the necessary power that is lacking. In order for you to increase your mastery of each power, *you must do them regularly!*

It is up to you how you decide to work on them. You could devote all your time on the third largest leg or start with the smallest leg. You may decide on a good regimen of daily exercises that divides your time among two or three of them.

For instance, if you feel that you excel in physical strength and lack focus, you may want to consider adding meditation and other concentration exercises to your routine. Or, if you feel you lack flexibility, you may want to do yoga and notice how important it is for you to be "right". If you find it hard to stick to your own point of view, you may want to take some time to bury your feet in the sand to ground yourself.

CLOSING STEPS
(see APPENDIX ONE on page 283 for details)
▷ **Shake out and stretch your legs**
▷ **Make notes on what you have discovered**

RECOMMENDED SCHEDULE
You only need to do this exercise once, but you may want to do it a couple of times to see if your evaluation of yourself changes. Once you have assessed yourself and established a clear practice, stick to it. After a period of time, like six months or a year, you could do a new assessment and see if you want to change your practice to suit your current needs.

TIPS

When I do this with clients, they sometimes gasp in shock when they see what they have drawn. When your four pillars are not equal, you are not living according to your true potential and tapping into your innate resources, power, and gifts. Your lack of balance is holding you back from manifesting your dreams, finding true happiness, and living in harmony with yourself and the world around you.

The point is not to discourage yourself, but to offer guidelines for what you need to do to develop your own stable, personal power. Your illustration of your table provides you with a personal portrait of who you currently are. Like any portrait that is taken of you, as you get older you no longer look like you did when that portrait was made. See it as a snapshot of this moment and know that you now have the tools to change and grow into the person you would like to be.

You may want to keep developing the pillars that you are already proficient at. I would say that it is good to maintain your mastery, but it would be a better use of your time to focus on the others where you lack proficiency. *The goal is to get the four legs to be equal in length.* If you think about it, a table with very short legs will still function as long as all the legs are equal. The power lies in the stability of the table, not how wide or long the legs are.

If you spend time on all four pillars and get them closer to an equal level of skill, you will become physically healthy, live your life with confidence, have the relationships you desire, and feel a sense of purpose and satisfaction in all that you do. You will reach your goals and be able to engage with all beings in any situation with confidence and skill.

In this section, we have explored the practices and steps necessary to develop as a confident, respectful, and responsible individual. Courageous Self-Reflection, setting clear motivations and values, becoming centered and present, and developing the Four Pillars of True Power prepare you for the subsequent parts of Respectful Confrontation. These include engaging with others, asserting your truth, and defending yourself and others from harm and conflict.

EXAMPLE OF
RESPECTFUL CONFRONTATION

EMPLOYEE	**Mr. Jackson?**
MANAGER	**Yes?**
EMPLOYEE	**I'm here for our meeting to talk about my raise.**
MANAGER	**Oh yeah. I'd love to talk with you about that, but I'm busy with this report.**
EMPLOYEE	**What report?**
MANAGER	**Albertson got in touch to say they need it this Friday.**
EMPLOYEE	**Wow, I can imagine you are feeling pressured. But just to check, you already agreed that I would be getting a raise, right?**
MANAGER	**Yes, we already discussed that.**
EMPLOYEE	**Great. Well, in that case I think we will only need about ten to fifteen minutes to discuss the details. How about we sit now for ten minutes or so to talk about the raise, and then I'm sure I can free up the rest of the morning to help you out with the report?**
MANAGER	**I don't know. I can't think about anything else right now. Let's talk about it next week.**
EMPLOYEE	**We already postponed talking about this last week and scheduled to talk about it now.**

MANAGER	Well, you know the nature of our work. Pressure and deadlines. We can't anticipate what will come up!
EMPLOYEE	I understand that, and I believe I function well with the pressure. That is why you are offering me a raise.
MANAGER	Okay, let's talk about it while we sort out these files.
EMPLOYEE	Mr. Jackson, this raise is very important to me. I'd like to have your full attention. As I said, I think we only need about ten to fifteen minutes to discuss this; I've laid out all the points. As soon as we are done, I will help you for the rest of the morning with the report.
MANAGER	Okay, great. I could use the help. Have a seat.
EMPLOYEE	Oh, okay.

ELLEN'S STORY

In the past, I saw myself as a weak person, both physically and in terms of will. I had a lack of assertiveness and was often indecisive. Respectful Confrontation helped me to realize that I am in fact far stronger in will and that I have a presence that is larger than my physical self. I also realized that I had been taking advantage of others' impressions of me as frail in order to elicit pity and avoid confrontation. I needed to confront my own attitude about myself in order to effectively communicate with others.

As a black woman, power to me meant privilege afforded by people of a certain race, gender, and stature. I adamantly decided from a young age that I would not react to my perceived lack of power as a black woman by getting angry, but I had yet to find a middle ground between being nagging and being a doormat. I've come to realize that in doing so, I've "given away" my power by leaving decisions up to others, not trying to change my situation, and feeling that others' opinions are more informed and carry more weight than my own.

Respectful Confrontation helped me open to my body awareness, my creativity, and my adaptability. Most importantly, through the simple exercises, I discovered my own inner strength and willpower. The "'Hey' Exercise" helped me to find my full voice. The grounding techniques, such as "Elephant Walking" and centered, deep breathing, helped me to tap into my values, beliefs, and true power in difficult situations.

I am able to apply these guidelines to every aspect of my life and practice the exercises at home. It has helped me interact well in the workplace and allowed me to better take care of myself throughout major life changes. I've also noticed the common thread of grounding, body awareness, personal power, and compassion in my life. I feel free! Free from the limitations I had unconsciously imposed upon myself.

I can't tell you how good it feels to be free of these. I can now see myself as a powerful black woman in a way that is true to my heart.

KEY POINTS

COURAGEOUS SELF-REFLECTION

.... ✓

SELF-EXAMINATION   PERSONAL GROWTH

RADICAL HONESTY   RESPECT

MOTIVATION

.... ✓

PURPOSE   GOALS

VALUES   OATH

PRESENCE & CENTEREDNESS

.... ✓

SELF-AWARENESS   LISTENING

NOTICING

FOUR PILLARS OF TRUE POWER

.... ✓

GROUNDING   FLEXIBILITY

FOCUS   MASCULINE AND FEMININE PRINCIPLES

STRENGTH

TOPICS FOR CONTEMPLATION OR JOURNALING

── ?

- *Why are you reading this book?*
- *What does personal freedom mean to you?*
- *What is your intention and goal as a Respectful Confronter?*
- *What are your core values? What motivates you? What will bring you fulfillment?*
- *How well do you notice and listen?*
- *What is your relationship with power? Positive? Negative? Neutral?*
- *How skillful are you with each of the Four Pillars of True Power?*
- *What practices will help you develop grounding, focus, strength, and flexibility?*

MASTERING RESPECTFUL CONFRONTATION

THE PRACTICE OF
RESPECTFUL ENGAGEMENT

THE DILEMMA

AMY   Hey, Lisa, are we still going to dinner tonight?

LISA   Yeah, definitely.

AMY   Okay, great. I would like to go to that nice Italian place.

LISA   No, I would rather have Chinese.

AMY   We always have Chinese. Let's do the Italian.

LISA   We don't always do Chinese. You always want Italian.

AMY   If I recall, we eat more Chinese than anything else.

LISA   That's not true.

AMY   Why are you making a big deal about this? You like Italian; I like Italian. Let's just eat Italian.

LISA   Because I want Chinese tonight.

AMY   I heard you. And I want Italian.

LISA   Fine, let's have Italian!

AMY   Fine!

LISA   Whatever...

"Getting my kids to do something was impossible. I used to just scream at them without really connecting. I now have ways to get them to listen. We may not always agree and we may still have arguments, but at least I feel that they know it's important to communicate with me instead of shutting off."

MAKING CONTACT

At the heart of Respectful Confrontation is the act of engaging with others in both loving and challenging situations. In this section, we will take a look at what *confrontation* is and how it is different from *conflict*. We will also examine ways to be successful in making an impactful connection with others as well as explore the structure and rules of effective communication.

When the beginning martial artist has proven herself through diligence, perseverance, respect, honor, and opening to the skills of the Four Pillars of True Power, the teacher will share with her the techniques and philosophies of fighting. The teacher always starts with how to stand facing an opponent, usually in the form of a bow, how to end a match with an opponent, usually with a bow, and the basic moves and principles of combat. The student will learn the importance of always staying connected to her opponent and finding ways to stay in the match as long as possible with both offensive and defensive moves.

The Respectful Confronter goes through a similar process. However, while the martial artist uses fighting to engage with her partner, the Respectful Confronter uses communication. In fact, you could say that Respectful Confrontation is nothing more than a sophisticated, skillful, and empowered form of communication. *Effective, empowered communication—following through with speaking your truth—is the way in which you collaborate and resolve conflicts.*

In this section, the Practice of Respectful Engagement, you will explore how to truly engage with another and ensure that a connection has been made; you will look at all the many layers of communication—from shallow verbal communication to the more subtle, deeper, non-verbal ways that we interact.

Engaging with another starts with making contact, which is the foundation and entranceway for all the subsequent practices in this book. Simply being in the same room with someone or using the familiar "How are you?" may be a way to start the interaction, but it doesn't mean you have truly made contact. In fact, these ways of engaging usually lead to misunderstandings and arguments. Just think about the frustration and misunderstandings that arise when you try to talk to someone who is watching TV, or even someone who may be looking at you but you can feel that their thoughts are somewhere else. This is not true engagement.

An effective way to truly make contact includes standing face-to-face with another person, connecting from your center (your personal power), from your heart (your understanding), with your eyes open, and listening with more than just your ears. When you engage with someone in this way, chances are you avoid misunderstanding and find exciting ways to collaborate and solve problems. Engaging with presence and authenticity allows you both to connect from your humanity where "you" and "I" merge to become "we".

No matter how good a martial artist is at kicking, punching or defending herself, she will never succeed if she hasn't taken the time to make that initial contact. The same is true with Respectful Confrontation. All the tools and strategies to create collaboration and overcome conflicts won't have any effect if you don't start by making contact and truly engaging with the other from a place of power and understanding.

Let's look at an exercise that will help you understand how to truly make contact. Ideally it would be helpful to do this exercise with someone or a group of people who are also reading this book and studying the practices. If you do this exercise with someone who is not reading the book, take the time to explain what the goal is of this exercise and take him through the steps. It may take a few times to really get into a good concentration with your partner. Remember, no judgments, just evaluate.

When you practice this with a partner, many distractions may come to the surface. To connect in such an open way means you are taking big emotional risks. This requires the courage to stay connected.

If you choose to do this exercise alone, you can practice with a mirror. It may seem strange to do this with your own mirror image, but it is a good preparation for making contact with others. Any mirror is fine, as long as you can see your face. The best would be a full-length mirror where you can see your whole body. Set up the mirror in a room where you won't be disturbed.

EXERCISE
MAKING CONTACT

**BEFORE YOU START THIS EXERCISE, REVIEW THE SECTION
"HOW TO USE THIS BOOK" ON PAGE 23**

PRELIMINARY STEPS

(see APPENDIX ONE on page 281 for details)

▷ **Choose a good time and location**

▷ **Start with the basic standing pose**

If you have trouble standing for a long time, start with the basic sitting pose. You should both do the same pose.

▷ **Bring your attention to your center**

▷ **Place all of your attention on your breath**

MAIN STEPS

▶ **Connect with the center of your partner, with their place of personal power**

While you are connecting with yourself, you are also standing or sitting opposite your partner. With your eyes closed, imagine approximately where your partner's center is. From your center, connect your awareness with the center of your partner. There is no need to touch; do this with your awareness.

Don't try to figure out how this should be done. Just try it. With your eyes closed, see if you can bring your awareness to your center and from your center see what it would be like to connect with the center of the other person. Hold that focus for a while. Notice any feelings.

Let this connection be the foundation of this interaction—like the foundation of a house.

▸ **Bring your awareness to your heart, the place of understanding and compassion**

Allow your awareness to rise up to your heart or a place in the middle of your chest. See how it feels to bring your focus to this area with the slightest bit of awareness still on your center. See what feelings come up or if energy flows.

▸ **Connect with the heart of your partner**

After a few moments, connect your heart with the heart of your partner. Remember, the best way to do this is to keep your eyes closed and there is no need to touch. Having connected your center of personal power with that of the person across from you, you now add your heart—your place of understanding and compassion—to that connection. Breathe into your heart and notice what feelings come up.

▸ **Slowly open your eyes and let your awareness from your center and heart flow to your partner**

Now that you have a connection from a level of personal power mixed with a connection from your heart, let that awareness flow up further to your eyes. Slowly open your eyes and make a connection with the eyes of the person across from you. Notice your feelings and any sensations. Don't hold back any reactions, emotions or flow of energy. See how this very conscious, open interaction affects you.

▸ **Stay in this connection, noticing how you and the other person are influencing each other**

Keep breathing and noticing. Stay connected from your eyes, your center, and your heart. Notice your level of presence, your openness, the strength of your contact, and how much you see and feel. If you are feeling tight in your body, let yourself relax into the connection more. If you feel expansion and flow, breathe into that and see what happens. Notice how vulnerable, how powerful or how uncomfortable you may feel. *Notice how you are influencing your partner and how your partner is influencing you.*

▸ **Practice staying connected and overcoming distractions that break the connection**

Let reactions occur, like giggling, tears, or tightness in breath. Notice it all and let it flow. Notice any impulse to turn away and end this interaction, and any judgments or distractions. Having an awareness of these patterns now will come in handy when engaging in real situations with others, especially when the interactions are challenging.

▸ **Notice your thoughts and assumptions**

As you continue to gaze at your partner, notice all your thoughts and all the assumptions you are making about this person standing across from you. Even if you are looking in a mirror, pay attention to the thoughts and judgments you are having about yourself. There's no need to judge yourself for having these thoughts; we all have them. Just notice. Here are some examples: *What a bad hairstyle. He really doesn't know how to dress. Oh, there's that needy look again. Her eyes are baggy; she must be tired. I wish I had green eyes. He is so big; it's scaring me.*

▸ **Put judgments and assumptions aside**

Remind yourself that all of these assumptions have nothing to do with the person. They are simply your own story of who this person is and what is going on. And be aware that these assumptions are creating distance and getting in the way of truly connecting.

See this person in this very moment and not based on your assumptions of the past or future. See this person, even yourself, with new eyes.

▸ **Stay connected and breathe into the feelings and the energy of this connection until you are done with the exercise**

CLOSING STEPS

(see APPENDIX ONE on page 283 for details)

▷ **Shake out and stretch your legs**

▷ **Make notes on what you have discovered**

▷ **Evaluate with your partner**

After you make notes, share your experience with your partner. Talk about what you learned and the challenges and discoveries you encountered.. There is no need to go too much into what actually happened; it's more important to evaluate and share what you learned and discovered. And make sure you don't judge yourself or the other person! Evaluate.

RECOMMENDED SCHEDULE

Take at least fifteen minutes to do this exercise, at least three times a week. Do this with one person or find a few people to do this with to see how it changes from person to person. *This exercise is the entranceway for all of the subsequent Respectful Confrontation practices, so I suggest you practice it often until it becomes a new habit.*

 TIPS

If you do this exercise a few times, you will get a clearer understanding of how to engage successfully. The more you do the exercise, the quicker it will become a new, healthy, empowering habit, and your interactions with others will have more flow, balance, and depth. You will have a strong impact on others, improving your relationships and efficacy at work. People will naturally be drawn to you and want to hear what you have to say.

True engagement includes connecting to your own personal and heart power, connecting to the personal and heart power of another, and listening with your full awareness. It then requires staying in this connection even if you feel the urge to break it, get distracted or feel uncomfortable with the vulnerability, the honesty, the challenges, and the misunderstandings that come up. The Respectful Confronter feels confident and skillful to stay engaged until the interaction comes to a logical, respectful, and mutual conclusion.

The success of your confrontations will depend on your skill and ability to stay engaged, especially when the confrontations are challenging and emotionally charged.

"Now that I have a new view of confrontation, that it is not conflict, I feel like I now have permission to say things I have always wanted to say. In the past, all my difficult conversations ended in an argument. Now, every time I think the other person will start fighting, they actually understand me."

CONFRONTATION, STANDING FACE-TO-FACE

Confrontation is essential for growth, progress, and transformation. This initial connection with another is the first moment that precedes the dance of life—collaboration, inspiration, and positive change. I like to break down the word confrontation into parts, con–front–ation, as a way to understand the true essence of the word. "Con" meaning "with." "Front" meaning "front". I like to say that the real meaning of confrontation is "With–front–open." This is a moment of extreme vulnerability when your true power is most present.

When you confront, you stand opposite someone and engage with your whole self—body, heart, and mind. Connecting with someone in this way will ensure that you and the other will mutually impact each other. *You can gauge just how open you need to be and how much you can let the other in without losing yourself.* By opening this way, with respect and understanding, something is exchanged; you are open to creativity and the flow of ideas and action. Anything is possible.

In essence, Respectful Confrontation is a mode of communication that is both compassionate and empowering, that is both assertive and vulnerable, and that allows for speaking and hearing truth. When you use this system, you will deepen your impact on the world in a positive way, both in your small personal circles and on a larger scale.

CONFRONTATION VS. CONFLICT

Every time a martial artist stands across from his opponent, he makes himself vulnerable and also honors the courageous spirit of the one he is opposing. Although both want to win, they acknowledge that the better they fight and step into their true power, the more they recognize and call upon the true power of the other.

The goal of fighting your best doesn't always have to come from a need to break your partner. You want to win the match, but by giving your "personal best", you challenge your partner in a way that allows him to grow and mature. This is what I call "benevolent competition". Yes, competition, and pushing beyond limits and fears, is a healthy part of the growth of an individual and of a society. However, this needs to be done in the spirit of cooperation and respect. International humanitarian and former U.S. president Jimmy Carter said, "Unless both sides win, no agreement can be permanent."

Current events around the world have shown that the old system of "win at all costs" is no longer being tolerated. The news is filled with accounts of how the strategies of disempowering your opponents, stepping on others to achieve your goals, and succeeding at all costs have brought our society into economic stress and many global conflicts. Former U.S. president George W. Bush, while giving a speech in 2001, highlighted a centuries-old edict that continues to cause more divisiveness and conflict with his statement, "Either you are with us or you are with the terrorists." This "win/lose" mentality, or competition with no scruples, causes a breakdown in many relationships and the disempowerment of many people.

Benevolent competition, the spirit behind Respectful Confrontation, leads to the deepening of relationships and the growth of all involved. If Mr. Bush and the leaders of the coalition had considered listening to the opinions of others and had found diplomatic ways to work with the Arab nations and deal with the rise of fundamentalist attacks, we may have been able to avoid the invasion of Iraq, torture in Guantanamo Bay, and the escalation of terrorist threats.

Webster's Dictionary defines CONFRONTATION in the following way:

Con·front ETYMOLOGY: Middle French *confronter* to border on, confront; from Latin *com-* + *front, frons,* forehead, front;

1   to face especially in challenge: OPPOSE 2 a: to cause to meet: bring face-to-face <*confront* a reader with statistics>

2   b: to meet face-to-face : ENCOUNTER <*confronted* the possibility of failure>

Notice how the definition focuses mostly on the idea of bringing face-to-face or to encounter. There seems to be an absence of malice or ill will.

Now take a look at how Webster's Dictionary defines CONFLICT:

Con·flict ETYMOLOGY: Middle English, from Latin *conflictus* act of striking together, from *confligere* to strike together, from *com-* + *fligere* to strike—more at PROFLIGATE;

1   FIGHT, BATTLE, WAR;

2   a: competitive or opposing action of incompatibles; antagonistic state or action (as of divergent ideas, interests or persons)

b: mental struggle resulting from incompatible or opposing needs, drives, wishes, or external or internal demands; **synonym** see DISCORD.

Do you see the difference? *Confrontation* is simply a way to engage; *conflict* leads to discord.

Recognizing the differences between these two concepts is the fundamental basis of the practice of Respectful Confrontation. In order for you to find personal freedom and have a positive, peaceful impact on those around you, you must first change your belief that confrontation and conflict are the same thing. They are not! Yes, both imply that two forces stand opposite each other, that some encounter will happen, and that both parties will experience some level of challenge. But the difference in the two lies in the motivation and the ultimate goal.

Here is how they are different from the perspective of Respectful Confrontation:

The goal of conflict is to break down the relationship, to create separation, and to gain power through the disempowerment of the other. The goal of confrontation is to deepen the relationship, to create closer connection, and to empower everyone involved.

By looking at it from this point of view, you could say that they are totally opposite from one another. On some level, conflict is easy. When you are in conflict—when there is separation—you get to be "right" or be a victim. You keep a distance from anyone or anything that may threaten your way of viewing the world. It is safe and convenient to surround yourself with others who will always agree with you; you never have to grow or be challenged.

The intention of confrontation is to bring individuals closer together, to deepen relationship, and to empower all involved. To confront implies that you are ready to stand before someone in an openhearted way, have the courage to speak your truth, and run the risk that you may be rejected or laughed at. It means that you are willing to hear the truth of another, even if his truth hurts your ego or may force you to shift your own way of thinking. It means having the right balance of assertiveness and flexibility to assure that you stay engaged even when emotions and unconscious behavior threaten the connection.

Why do we have so much trouble confronting and engaging in this openhearted way? *Because engaging in this way is uncomfortable.* Standing across from someone with presence and vulnerability is a loaded moment where anything can happen. Former prime minister of Israel, Yitzhak Rabin said, "We must think differently, look at things in a different way. Peace requires a world of new concepts, new definitions."

Standing face-to-face in your vulnerability in order to engage with the humanity of another requires a warrior spirit and the skills of Respectful Confrontation. Each person you encounter will receive your attention, and you will utilize your true power to navigate any struggles in the same honorable way that a martial artist engages with an opponent. The more you know how people interact with one another in a variety of situations, the more mindfully you will use that interaction for the benefit of all involved.

The power of openhearted engagement is now being scientifically measured. The Institute of HeartMath, a non-profit research organization that has been studying the electromagnetic energy generated by emotions, the body, and the heart, can now directly measure an energy exchange between people.

According to the research, "The heart generates the strongest, rhythmic, electromagnetic field generated in the body. Measured with modern magnetic field meters, the heart's electromagnetic field is approximately five thousand times greater in strength than the field produced by the brain. The heart's field permeates every cell in the body and radiates up to eight feet outside the body." With this ratio of heart to brain, you can imagine how influential you could be when you approach others in an openhearted, empowered way and not only from your thoughts and opinions.

Sounds ideal, doesn't it? It almost sounds too good to be true. Well, it *is* possible and requires courage, new attitudes, new commitments, and learning new skills; it also means overcoming many old judgments, fears, and false viewpoints. Martin Luther King, Jr. said, "Man must evolve for all human conflict a method which rejects revenge, aggression, and retaliation. The foundation of such a method is love."

PRACTICING CONFRONTATION

What do you think about this way of viewing confrontation and conflict? Think of moments in your life when you were in conflict with someone and when you were in confrontation. Make it a practice to remember this concept for a day or two and notice how you engage with others.

- *Do you seek out connection?*
- *Do you keep your distance and use confusion as a way to maintain a sense of control?*
- *Do you put yourself in uncomfortable situations in order to get to the heart of issues or do you pull away when you are confronted?*
- *Do you choose not to speak your truth or ask for what you need, in order to "keep the peace"?*
- *Do you keep silent about something even if it means that someone else may suffer?*

Be honest and don't judge yourself. We have all done the things I've mentioned above.

The point is for you to get a sense of what the differences are when you use conflict or confrontation in any given situation. What is most important is that you get a strong sense of how it *feels* to do one or the other. Confrontation should feel more uncomfortable, but ultimately lead to an open, expansive, and connected feeling. However, this is counter-intuitive; our basic nature is to seek out comfort. *If you can train yourself to feel at home in uncomfortable situations, you will see positive results.* Conflict may not feel uncomfortable, it may even feel powerful on some level, but ultimately it leads to a constricted, cut-off feeling. By feeling it strongly, you become more aware of your patterns and have the ability to correct yourself and grow.

When you separate conflict from confrontation, you become more conscious of your own behavior and change your life and the lives of those around you. You avoid creating conflict and commit to confronting yourself and others with the purpose of deeper connection and growth, and you feel confident to speak your truth knowing that your motivation is to empower all involved.

There are many reasons why we avoid confrontation and fall into the habit of creating conflict:

- *Some of us choose conflict because we were taught it is the only way. When we don't question our beliefs or examine our motives, we typically engage with our reactive, unconscious behavior and aggression*

- *Many of us who would like to avoid conflict also avoid confrontation because somehow we believe that they are the same. We choose to live our lives not speaking our truths and being in our power. We watch conflict and strife happen around us and do nothing because we think that if we did something about them, we would only contribute to the confusion and separation. This makes sense if you believe the two are the same*

- *Confrontation is hard work. Choosing to engage with vulnerability and presence requires a skillful ability to "dance" with anything that may come up and ensure that the connection remains open and doesn't shut down. If you think about it, whether in a sweet, intimate moment with someone or in a challenging discussion, there is always the risk that the connection will break down and the heart will close.*

*This is when misunderstandings occur, when deeper rifts develop,
and where conflict begins*

- *Being nice and "keeping the peace at all costs" is another way to
avoid confrontation. This commonplace, unconscious tactic also leads
to conflict. Yes, it is important to be loving and good to others and
yourself; sometimes being nice is a great way to connect. But I don't
think being nice is the answer for all situations. Those who are stuck
in a "nice guy" mentality avoid asking for what they need or asserting
their power, remain unhappy, and wish that things could be better*

"Nice guys", both men and women, think that their only two options
for engaging with others are being nice or being hurtful. This is not true.
Confrontation is needed when being nice doesn't accomplish the goal;
this means that sometimes you may have to say things to someone that
the other may not think are very nice. But let's not forget the goal of
confrontation is to deepen relationship, create closeness, and empower
the other. Sounds good to any "nice guy", right?

Be clear on your motivation when you confront someone that you
know will get upset or hurt because you are daring to speak your truth
or try to help that person through some difficult issues. This will help
you to follow through. Jimmy Carter said, "If you fear making anyone
mad, then you ultimately probe for the lowest common denominator of
human achievement."

Think of a situation where someone continually gives money to a
friend even though this friend is going to use that money for drugs. The
"nice guy" will keep giving the money, right? Even though giving the
money is causing harm, the "nice guy" doesn't want to rock the boat,
hurt the feelings of the other person or tarnish a strong, "nice guy"
reputation.

But is continuing to give the money empowering the other person? No. Is it deepening the relationship and bringing the two of them closer? No, because the "nice guy" is probably seething with resentment and worry, and the other is dropping deeper into his problems and isolation. Actually, in this case, you could say that acting like the "nice guy" and enabling the problem is creating conflict!

What is called for is Respectful Confrontation. At some point, the "nice guy" could stop giving the money, even though this will definitely cause pain, anger, and many other unpleasant reactions. Being truly compassionate sometimes leads to initial pain, but speaking your truth may result in the healing and empowerment of the other. You replace "nice" with compassionate power, the true force of the Respectful Confronter.

Approaching each encounter with courage, taking a risk so that a deepening of trust can take place, is the power of vulnerability and confrontation. In the end, both parties will have changed their views on an issue or overcome a problem, leading to the empowerment of each one involved.

This is a challenging process that demands true power and skill since many people you will come in contact with are different from you, may not want to engage with you or may trigger your own reactive behavior. You are not going to walk around with a wide open heart all the time. That is not very smart and could cause problems and pain. Keen awareness and wisdom are needed to assess how open the other is and how open you are willing to be to engage and still take care of yourself.

In order to avoid and resolve misunderstandings and the breakdown of relationship, you need a veritable arsenal of skills to address the myriad of ways humans interact. Before we discuss how to assert your truth and react to the behavior of others, we must first look at the intricacies of communication and the subtle ways we engage and influence one another.

"I always saw myself as a good communicator. But with these new insights I notice how I wasn't addressing the more important aspects of my relationships. Now I feel more relaxed with my wife and I am saving a lot of time at work. My sales are up!"

MASTERING RESPECTFUL CONFRONTATION

UNDERSTANDING COMMUNICATION

As soon as you start engaging with someone, an intricate system of communication gets activated. Before the martial artist learns how to block and attack, he first needs to understand the rules of combat and foundations of fighting. Similarly, the next step for the Respectful Confronter is to understand the rules and structure of communication.

Because Respectful Confrontation is *nothing more than empowered communication*, it is essential to look closely at how people interact, as well as the different layers of communication, both verbal and non-verbal. To communicate successfully, one needs to acknowledge that human interaction is a lot more complex than the words that are spoken. When you engage with others, you are engaging with their whole being, the things that are easy to see, as well as the parts that are present but not obvious to identify.

We may all know how to communicate; yet we still manage to mess it up with misunderstandings and assumptions that cause conflict and stress. Let's take a look at some very simple yet powerful tools and practices to ensure we minimize miscommunication and succeed in avoiding and resolving conflict. We will first take a look at the structure of communication, then look at the hidden aspects of communication, and finally examine how behaviors, needs, and feelings influence our interactions.

FIVE STEPS TO CLEAR COMMUNICATION

Let's start with the basic structure of communication. Think about how you communicate. Speaking to others may seem easy, especially when you talk to people you know who speak the same language and who have no physical challenges that impede their ability to hear or see. You would think with so few obstacles that all your conversations would be successful. Right?

Wrong. We still manage to be unclear so our message is not received in a way that we intended it. Before we know it, our innocent statement leads to a huge misunderstanding. This happens over and over again, and we can't seem to control it. However, by knowing the structure and intricacies of communication, we minimize misunderstandings and actually use communication as a powerful tool for growth, peace, and collaboration.

Let's look at an example. Suppose Peter and Rachel are at home hanging out. Peter says to Rachel, "I would like a cup of tea." Rachel stands up and says, "I can't believe you said that," and storms out of the room, angry. What happened? Was that a successful communication? Unless the motivation of Peter was to upset Rachel, I would say that the communication was unsuccessful.

If the communication had been clear, here are three possibilities for how Rachel could respond: "Yeah, now that you mention it, I would like one too. Make one for me as well." Or, "That sounds great. I'll go make it for you." Or, "Oh yeah, great. Not me. No time to make it."

So where did the communication go wrong? There are many possibilities, but let's first investigate the actual structure of communication to see if we can find the culprit. Since most of us have been talking for many years, we take it for granted that just saying something is enough to ensure that our message gets across. There is more to it. When our communication is clear, we go through five steps, whether we know it or not. One reason we fail in our communication is because we tend to skip one or more of these five steps.

FIVE STEPS TO CLEAR COMMUNICATION

....

(1) CONTACT WITH YOURSELF

To ensure that your communication is clear, you first need to become present and centered. Look at the exercises in Section One to find out ways to do this.

(2) CONTACT WITH OTHER

You then make contact with the other person, either with eye contact or some other way to have full engagement. This means that both parties are present, open, and there is a flow. Take a look at the exercise in this section called "Making Contact" on page 122 to get a better grasp of what it means to fully engage.

(3) DESIRE/IMPULSE

At this point, you feel a need, a desire, a feeling, an impulse or an intention to communicate something. In our scenario, Peter desires a cup of tea and feels compelled to share that with Rachel. In other cases it might be something like "What are you doing for dinner?" Or, "Watch out for the bus!" Or, "You're standing in front of the TV!"

④ ACT OF COMMUNICATING

Now that you are present, you have contact with the other, and you feel the impulse, you communicate what is desired. This can be with words, a gesture, a sound, facial expressions or any other way that your message can be clearly communicated.

⑤ RECEIVED MESSAGE

After communicating what you feel compelled to share, *you wait to see if your message was received!* This confirmation that your message was received can be a gesture, words, a look, a nod or some kind of acknowledgment from the other. That person doesn't have to agree with you, but all you need to know is that you were successful in getting the message across.

I believe that this fifth step is the most important of all five and the one that is often skipped. You could say that much of our conflicts are caused by our forgetting to see if what we are communicating was received in the way we meant or was even received at all.

. . . .

How many times have you caught yourself saying, "I tell him over and over again to do it and he never does." It may be that he just doesn't want to do it, but it could also be that he didn't really hear what you were saying because he was distracted or emotionally disconnected from you. We assume that what seems clear to us will be clear to others. This is a big mistake!

Think about how you communicate. Do you go through all five steps when you talk to others? Can you recognize which of the five steps you tend to skip over the most? Take the time in the next couple of days, at work or with your family, to think about these steps as you engage with others. Notice how you use or don't use these five steps in your conversations. Are you using the right amount of force and precision along with the five steps? (This would be a good time to review the "'Hey' Exercise" on page 82 in the chapter on The Four Pillars of True Power)

Steps 3 and 4 are very familiar to us—especially Step 4. We can easily feel an impulse to communicate something and then say it. In fact, we all know people who can keep Step 4 going for a long, long time. Talking, talking, and talking. But are they really being heard or understood? Are they present? Most likely, the other has tuned out; there is no contact and the message is not being received.

There may be many reasons why there is a lack of clear communication. Maybe your message wasn't focused enough or was too weak; maybe you weren't fully present or didn't check to see if you had contact with the other. Maybe you didn't check in with yourself to see what you really wanted to say. Or maybe you were already running out the door before you checked to see if the other really understood what you meant. Who knows? *As a Respectful Confronter, you recognize your own patterns and make choices to improve your skills.*

In challenging confrontations, Steps 1, 2, and 5 are the most important to master. To first get yourself fully present and then make sure you are connecting with the other is essential in clear, openhearted communication. This can be annoying to the other and time consuming, but in the end you will save time doing this, knowing that you only have to say something once to get your point across.

When you skip these steps, you may have to start all over again, or you will discover that a project has gone wrong or you end up in an argument that can take days to resolve. Use your time well. *Start with centering yourself, being sure you have the full attention of the other, speak your truth, and then make sure your message is received.*

A martial artist will strike a blow, check its impact, and then wait to see how the other will react before strategizing the next move. When you confront, focusing on Step 5, knowing when and if your message was received, will inform you of what the next step could be. This is the give and take of communication.

When you master the Five Steps to Clear Communication, you will discover that you have more impact, you say less to get your point across, and that you spend less time arguing and dealing with unnecessary misunderstandings.

WHAT LIES UNDERNEATH COMMUNICATION

We have examined the five-step process that leads to clear communication. We now understand the rules of the game so we can stay in the game, even if the stakes are high. But even though we know the rules and execute all five steps successfully, there are always unseen forces that can throw us off and get in the way of giving and receiving clear messages.

Let's go back to our scenario with the cup of tea. Peter may have taken the time to center, make contact with the other, tap into the need, communicate it, and then wait for a response, but Rachel still stood up and stormed angrily out of the room. What went wrong? There was nothing in the words on the surface that would have triggered what seems like an irrational reaction from Rachel. Let's take a closer look.

If our communication was only based on our words, we would have less fighting and our communication would be more efficient like a computer. As long as you input the right data, a computer will never misinterpret what you are trying to communicate. A computer can only respond to the words or data that is being presented. But we are not machines; we are far more complex and intricate. Since the cause of the miscommunication wasn't the words or a breakdown in the engagement, it could have come from what was *under* the words.

When you find yourself in an argument or misunderstanding, and you are sure that your words and interactions are clear, dive down under the words. You will find a whole world of complexity, richness, and creativity. This world of the "non-verbal" is a familiar terrain for psychologists and researchers of human behavior. Sigmund Freud spoke about people as "a closed system of psychic energy that is floating between the conscious and the unconscious human spirit."

THE ICEBERG PRINCIPLE

In Brent D. Ruben's classic book from the 1970s, *Communication and Human Behavior*, he compares human communication with an iceberg. When you see an iceberg, you are only seeing about ten percent of that iceberg above the surface. Ninety percent of the iceberg is submerged under the water. Similarly, with human communication, the words themselves make up about ten percent, and ninety percent of our interaction is influenced by the parts of us that are not easily seen or recognized at first sight. *It is in the submerged, unconscious realm of our personalities that we most often find the causes of our misunderstandings and conflicts.*

When you know exactly what makes up this ninety percent of your interactions, it will be easier to avoid and resolve any problems that may arise due to these hidden factors. Let's put on our diving gear, jump in, and explore what is under the surface. Take a look at the following chart and see if you recognize these factors and how they influence your interactions. Notice that as you go lower on the iceberg, the unseen factors get more subtle and harder to detect. As we swim around and explore this dark world of rich and colorful personality traits, make it personal to you. See how each factor could color, influence, enhance, disrupt, and break down your communication, connection, and collaboration.

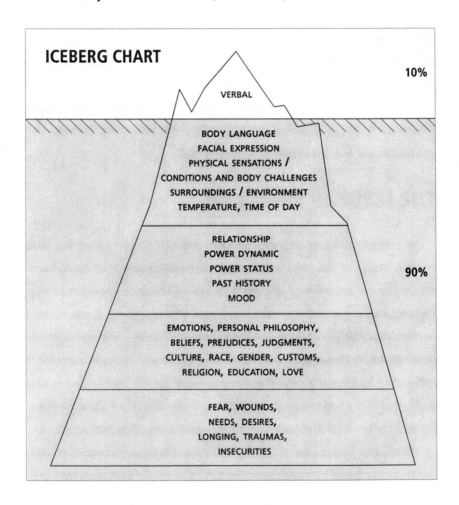

MASTERING RESPECTFUL CONFRONTATION

Wow, it is a rich and exciting world down there—just under the surface of how you present yourself to others and how you interact and engage. These factors are with you all the time and wherever you go! Do you recognize these elements in yourself and those around you? I'm sure you could come up with other unseen factors to add to this list that are more personal to you and your circumstances. For instance, when you see *beliefs*, what are your unique beliefs that influence your interactions? Can you identify your own personal *wounds* or *desires* and see how they could color how you engage with others?

Looking at our scenario with Peter and Rachel, ten percent of the interaction is in the words, "I would like a cup of tea." Let's say that Peter was successful in using all five steps to communicate. So, what could have possibly caused Rachel to storm angrily out of the room? Let's dive down and take a look. Maybe it had to do with the power dynamic of the relationship. Or maybe the idea of tea makes Rachel think about her beloved grandmother who just recently passed away and she was angry that Peter was so insensitive to mention tea at this time. These are just two possibilities. I'm sure you could come up with others.

Think about your interactions with others like friends and family, adversaries, and even strangers. Go to the supermarket and when you get to the check-out counter, take a moment to notice the interaction with the check-out person; be aware of all the factors that you bring to that encounter then think of all the possible factors they bring to it as well.

Practice this at all times. Do this at the dinner table. Nobody needs to know. Take a walk down a busy street. Be aware of the total you— all one hundred percent. Now be aware and feel the one hundred percent of everyone around you. What you discover is how rich and complex human beings are. This richness and complexity is the very thing that leads to growth and collaboration, but also has the capacity to destroy and break things down.

The point of closely examining these unseen forces is not to discourage you or make you think that you are an emotional mess, a victim to circumstance or that you are imprisoned by your patterns. On the contrary, *the more you develop an intimate relationship with your own unconscious self*, the more you can tap into the richness of who you are, celebrate the complexities of all these layers, and share that with the world in a creative way.

For the purpose of Respectful Confrontation, diving into the subtle realms of yourself and others *makes you aware of how fragile and delicate communication is*. Because there are so many factors that could lead to misunderstanding and throw you off balance in your engagement, it is essential to communicate in an authentic way and to really listen. This could motivate you to master the tools of Respectful Confrontation.

When you are not mindful and get into your reactive behavior, these unseen factors float to the surface and cause miscommunication and conflict. When the connection with yourself and another is ruptured or is on the brink of rupturing, it is up to you to find a way to stay engaged and search for the cause of the misunderstanding. The skill lies in the ability to specifically identify the underlying causes. First, dive down into your own ninety percent of unseen factors to see if you can find the cause. If you can't find it within yourself, investigate what unseen factors may have been triggered in the other. When you think you have found what might be the cause, bring it up to the surface and see if there is room to discuss it.

This may seem like a lot of work, but the more you practice this, the more it will become second nature. In the beginning, you may feel stilted or pressured. Keep it light. Get to know your own unseen factors. The more familiar they are to you, the less likely they will get the better of you in heated moments and pull you into your reactive behavior.

DEVELOPING THE VOCABULARY OF FEELINGS AND NEEDS

Now that you have learned the rules of communication (Five Steps to Clear Communication) and examined the intricacies of human interaction (the Iceberg Principle), it's time to actually see how fluent you are in the language of Respectful Confrontation. As stated before, to truly communicate in an empowered way, you must be willing to open to another with vulnerability. This openhearted engagement will lead to deepening of relationship, the empowerment of all involved, and the possible resolution of conflicts that in the past seemed impossible to solve.

This empowered vulnerability requires you to use words that are challenging or unknown to many. The more fluent you are in the language of feelings and needs, the deeper the connection and trust with others. Marshall Rosenberg, an American psychologist and the creator of Nonviolent Communication, believes that the key to healing, and even restorative justice, lies in the ability for individuals to communicate and honor their needs. He said, "Behind intimidating messages are simply people appealing to us to meet their needs. When we understand the needs that motivate our own and others' behavior, we have no enemies."

By speaking about your feelings and needs, the other gets a chance to see more of who you are and feel safe. This gives you both the freedom to speak your truth and to get your needs met, leading to more clarity in the relationship, personal freedom, and fulfillment.

You may have had moments with challenging discussions where there was openhearted connection and you were both willing to hear the other's truth. But then comes the moment when you are expected to express your feelings and needs. This is when many of us fumble.

There are many reasons why we fumble. Here are some:

- *Expressing feelings and needs takes us to a deeper level of vulnerability and risk-taking, which might be too frightening*
- *We have so many judgments and unexamined assumptions about expressing feelings and needs*
- *We just don't know how to get in contact with what we are feeling or needing*
- *We don't have a broad enough vocabulary to express exactly what we are feeling or needing*

Do you recognize this? Think about what we have been taught, especially in Western modern cultures. Many of us believe that expressing feelings and needs makes us weak or "needy". This belief is antithetical to the physical, emotional, mental, and spiritual health of any individual and a primary cause of stress, anxiety, illness, and the breakdown of relationship and culture. Brené Brown, an author, lecturer, and social worker, who researched vulnerability and authenticity for more than ten years, said, "In our culture we've come to equate success with not needing anyone. Studying wholeheartedness taught me this: until we can receive with an open heart, we are never really giving with an open heart. When we attach judgment to receiving help, we knowingly or unknowingly attach judgment to giving help."

For most men, expressing feelings and needs is almost an impossibility.

"Ya gotta be tough," my dad used to say. The "Lone Cowboy" image of the United States sums this up well. In the Old West, the cowboy survived on his own, didn't bond emotionally with others, and he took what he wanted instead of asking for what he needed. Actually, these men were really only as powerful as their guns and taking what they wanted usually ended in a gunfight. There was no room for openhearted connection in this environment. This is the old way!

In the new paradigm, you are empowered to express your feelings and needs. It is not possible for any being on this planet to fulfill all of his or her needs alone. Some things we can take care of ourselves, and for other things, we must reach out and ask for help. This is difficult for most adults to accept. *True power comes when you are able to identify what you need and then have the courage to reach out and ask others for support.*

Because of strong prejudices, shame, embarrassment, and fears about expressing feelings and needs, we were never really taught the appropriate vocabulary. And because we are not fluent in the language of feelings and needs, we avoid recognizing and expressing them.

Think about some of your deep conversations with friends, lovers, and work colleagues. When it comes to the point when you would like to express what you are feeling or needing, what happens? For many of us, we begin to stammer, search for words, and end up feeling embarrassed and helpless. Because this is a very uncomfortable moment, many of us end the discussion or change the subject.

However, this is the magical moment in intimacy, negotiation, and collaboration when a deepening of relationship and effectiveness in productivity can happen. When you can stay with the discomfort and express your feelings and needs, then you can move forward more quickly as a work team, couple or family.

WANTS VS. NEED

You may stay engaged and manage to find something to say, but instead of expressing what you *feel* or *need*, you settle for telling the other what you *think* or *want*. This may feel safer, but usually leads to a misunderstanding of expectations or an inability to come to a resolution. Have you ever heard someone say, "I *want* you to love me more." The problem with thoughts and wants is that they are often based on fantasies of the future, shaped by past pain and unexamined assumptions, and almost impossible to attain.

Expressing a thought or a want seems easier because it usually refers to something outside of yourself, puts the responsibility on the other to deal with the situation or is used as a clever way to avoid going deeper into your own truth. For instance, you may *want* the "perfect" lover (which nobody ever finds, of course), but what you really *need* today is someone to give you a hug and some encouragement. Your *opinion* may be that it is justified for someone to cancel at the last minute because they are working hard, but you actually *feel* disappointed. You may *want* your colleague to have the report done right now, but you really don't *need* it until the day after tomorrow.

Keeping your interactions on the level of thoughts and wants leads to confusion, misunderstanding, insufficient productivity, and wasted time. A want is something individual to the person and oftentimes is hard to comprehend. Needs, on the other hand, are more universal, and therefore easier for another to understand and connect with. For example, on some level, we all have felt the need to be seen, to feel secure, and to be acknowledged. By recognizing commonality, it is easier to support one another.

Let's go back to our scenario with Peter and Rachel to see if this new information can help us uncover the cause of Rachel's reaction: In a past conversation, Rachel fumbled with expressing her needs to Peter. All she could say was, "I want you to love me more." The request was too vague and based on fantasy. What can Peter possibly do to satisfy Rachel? If he had asked Rachel, "what does that look like?" or something similar, they could have avoided the conflict. Because Rachel expressed her thoughts and wants and not her needs, and Peter didn't ask for clarification, Peter feels powerless to satisfy his partner, and Rachel remains disappointed and angry. Both are engaging with a high level of anxiety and frustration at the moment when Peter mentions that he would like some tea.

Maybe that is why Rachel stormed off in anger! She thought she was clear about her needs. She assumed that Peter would know exactly what she needed. She was waiting for Peter to offer to make her a cup of tea. That would have been so romantic. However, instead of offering to make tea, all he said was, "I would like a cup of tea." He had the nerve to passively ask her to make him a cup of tea! She got angry and once again felt like she didn't get her needs met. Now we have uncovered the cause of the miscommunication. Rachel thought she was being clear in her communication, but Peter had no idea.

The best way to get past your thoughts and wants is to go within, use deeper listening, and ask yourself, "What am I feeling and needing right now?" This is always specific. Directly connected to truth and vulnerability, it usually results in the other opening up more and wanting to do his best to accommodate. When coming from clarity and not from confusion, it is easier for the other to decide if they are going to give you what you need or not.

Expecting others to know what you need is not fair. They are not mind readers. If they care about you, they may help you to figure it out, but it is up to you to take responsibility for expressing your own feelings and needs. Your spoken needs could be simple: *I need to be seen. I need nurturing. Would you be able to find one thing a day to do for me that will help me to feel seen and nurtured? It doesn't have to be anything more than a hug.*

PRACTICE IDENTIFYING YOUR FEELINGS AND NEEDS

How fluent are you in this language? Are you able to connect with your authentic self in both loving and challenging situations and communicate on a deeper level? Do an inventory. Notice all the words you use to describe your feelings and needs in your daily life. Are you using the same word all the time? Are you using general words, like "interesting", "fine" or "okay"? What words would be risky for you to use? Start making lists of your personal vocabulary of feelings and needs.

If you find yourself in a situation where you are asked to express your feelings and you don't know what to say, first check to see if what you are experiencing is either "pleasant" or "unpleasant". These two simple words will add a depth to your communication.

If you don't have many words on your list, take a look at the following lists. Study them. Add more words over a period of time until you compile a list with hundreds of feelings and needs. If you are truly committed to the skills of Respectful Confrontation and mastering empowered communication, memorize them.

Figure out the best way for you to memorize and practice these words. I always found the approach from elementary school useful. Take one word a day and then remember to use that one word as much as possible throughout the day. The more you use it, the more familiar it will become. When these new words become second nature, you will find yourself using them in your engagements with others, resulting in deeper, richer interactions.

FEELINGS

PLEASANT / UNPLEASANT

ALIVE	DESPERATE	INSPIRED	PLAYFUL
ANNOYED	DISAPPOINTED	INTERESTED	PUZZLED
APPRECIATIVE	ECSTATIC	IRRITABLE	SAD
CALM	EXCITED	JOYFUL	SATISFIED
CONFIDENT	FASCINATED	LONELY	SCARED
CONFUSED	FRUSTRATED	LOVING	SHOCKED
CONTENT	GLAD	MISCHIEVOUS	SUSPICIOUS
EMBARRASSED	HELPLESS	NERVOUS	TENDER
DESPAIRING	HURT	OVERWHELMED	TIRED

NEEDS

ACCEPTANCE	EQUALITY	TO KNOW	RESPECT
AUTHENTICITY	FLOW	LOVE	REST
BELONGING	FREEDOM	TO MATTER	SAFETY
CELEBRATION	GROWTH	MEANING	TO BE SEEN
CLARITY	HARMONY	ORDER	SUPPORT
COOPERATION	HONESTY	PLAY	SUSTENANCE
CREATIVITY	INFLUENCE	POWER	TOUCH
EASE	INTEGRITY	PROTECTION	UNDERSTANDING

In this section, The Practice of Respectful Engagement, you have covered the basic rules and intricacies of making contact, engaging with others, and communication. These theories and skills are necessary in order to take the next steps in the process of Respectful Confrontation, which include taking the offense to speak your truth, as well as mastering defensive strategies when your encounters get challenging or threatening. With Respectful Engagement, the openhearted game of personal expression and empowered collaboration has begun. In the next sections, the game gets very interesting!

EXAMPLE OF
RESPECTFUL CONFRONTATION

AMY   Hey, Lisa, are we still going to dinner tonight?

LISA   Yeah, definitely.

AMY   Okay, great. I would like to go to that nice Italian place.

LISA   No, I would rather have Chinese.

AMY   We always have Chinese. Let's do the Italian.

LISA   We don't always do the Chinese. If I recall, we eat more Italian than anything else.

AMY   We've gone to Chinese a lot lately because you keep suggesting we go there. I've had enough Chinese for a while.

LISA   Why are you making a big deal about this?

AMY   Lisa, what's going on? This is not like you. You seem on edge lately.

LISA   I don't want to talk about it. Let's go wherever you want.

AMY   No, what's going on?

LISA   I haven't wanted to bring it up. It is very embarrassing. I thought it would be solved by now.

AMY   What?

LISA   I got some big bills in lately that I didn't anticipate—federal taxes, car payments. I have to watch my money these days. I'm on a stricter budget.

AMY   I'm sorry to hear it.

LISA   I've been eating at home more often and trying to cut costs. The Italian is pretty expensive.

AMY   Wow, I didn't know.

LISA   So, what I need is to go to restaurants that are a bit cheaper. That's why we've been going to the Chinese restaurant so often. The prices are reasonable.

AMY   I'm so glad you told me what's going on and shared with me what you need. I don't mind going to other restaurants. I actually know of a good Italian restaurant that is not so pricey.

LISA   You really want Italian!

AMY   You know how much I like it. And also, I didn't want to tell you, but I am a bit sensitive to the MSG in the Chinese food. I usually get a headache after eating it.

LISA   Oh, I didn't know.

AMY   So, I need to take a break from the Chinese for a while.

LISA   Good to know. So, let's try that other Italian place. It sounds good.

AMY   Great. I also know some other really good restaurants with reasonable prices we should try.

LISA   Great. See you tonight.

AKAYLA'S STORY

Respectful Confrontation offered me a path to freedom! I wanted to find a way of communicating that did not dissolve into anger, despair, and cold silence. I wanted to be a model for my sons and their friends. I wanted communication tools that would allow me and my boys to hold on to our dignity, and let the other people we're dealing with in very difficult situations keep theirs. I now have access to feelings and memories that had been closed off to me.

Respectful Confrontation removed my fear of communicating. Without the fear, I am more aware of what is going on. I notice both the words and the "freeze, flight or fight" patterns. Instead of assailing or retreating, I am present when I speak with others and don't get lost in anger and despair. I have clarity, and with that clarity I am able to make decisions.

I am now more in touch with my own power. My response to "fight" and out of control communication is to state my position and/or my boundary and stay there. I am open, but not acquiescent. I no longer define "quiet" as peaceful. Being aware of my strengths has allowed me the confidence to reach out more.

Following the Respectful Confrontation principle of right time, right place, and right attitude, I approached my husband about the ongoing issues of his harsh/abusive speech directed at me. I told him how it makes me feel—sad, angry, attacked, and abused. I asked that he stop doing this because it has been poisonous to our relationship.

He seemed confused that I had set forth both the issue and my feelings about it without tears, anger or personal attack. I only dealt with the behavior. After being silent for a while, he stated that speaking that way was just how he is. I responded that he seemed to be able to speak politely with others. He countered with I'm always trying to make him the bad guy. I pointed out how he was treating me at that moment, naming the behavior. He responded that I was always laying something on him, and I should know how he is at this point. That was the end of the conversation.

Respectful Confrontation does not give me happy endings with my husband, but it does allow me to clearly see the issues. In this case, it clarified for me that my husband does not choose to recognize some very basic issues in our marriage. His "flight" behavior, through anger and misrepresentation, won't dissuade me from my need for clear communication and working things out over time. Knowing that allows me to make different choices and embrace my heart and life.

KEY POINTS

OPENHEARTED ENGAGEMENT ✓

MAKING CONTACT

CONFRONTATION

CONFLICT

FIVE STEPS TO CLEAR COMMUNICATION ✓

ONE HUNDRED PERCENT OF HUMAN INTERACTION ✓

VOCABULARY OF FEELINGS AND NEEDS ✓

TOPICS FOR CONTEMPLATION OR JOURNALING ❓

- *What does openhearted, empowered engagement mean to you?*
- *How connected do you feel to yourself, your surroundings, and others? Do you seek out connection?*
- *What does it feel like when you have really made contact with someone?*
- *What are your viewpoints on confrontation and conflict? What is your relationship with them?*
- *How well do you communicate? Do you use all of the Five Steps To Clear Communication?*
- *Can you identify the hidden factors in yourself and others that influence your communication?*
- *How fluent are you in the language of feelings and needs?*
- *How comfortable are you in expressing your feelings and needs?*

MASTERING RESPECTFUL CONFRONTATION

THE PRACTICE OF
RESPECTFUL
OFFENSE

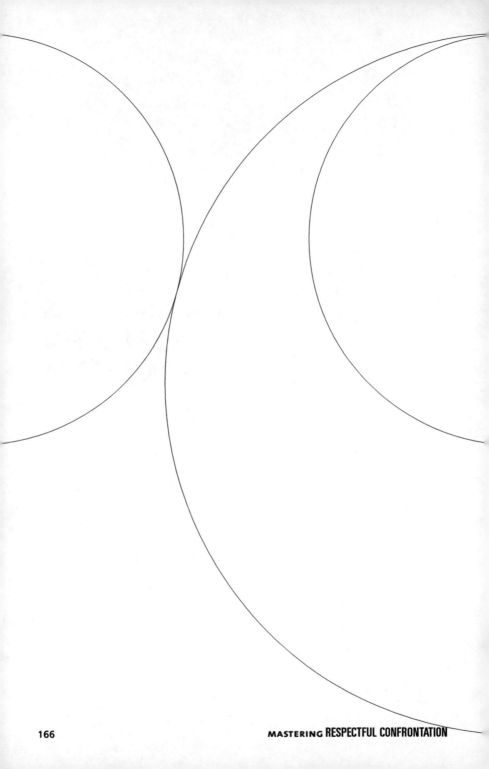

THE DILEMMA

JACK   Nina, we need to talk.

NINA   What is it? I'm really busy. Let's talk about it tomorrow.

JACK   No, I want to talk about it now.

NINA   Didn't you hear me? I don't want to talk about it now.
            I am busy with these emails.

JACK   This is important. You haven't done the dishes!

NINA   Are you kidding me? I can't be bothered with the dishes
            right now.

JACK   The place is a mess. I can't take it anymore. You agreed to
            do it!

NINA   I'm too busy! Do them yourself. Stop making a big deal
            about it. You always make a big deal about everything!

JACK   Well, if you did what you said you were going to do,
            then...

"I think I'm very good at asserting myself in the workplace, but when it comes to family and relationships I crumble. I am usually the quiet one who keeps the peace. However, I now see that I can use the same confidence in my work situation and use that with my family. It is not easy; it's sometimes scary. But I'm seeing slow progress."

UNDERSTANDING ASSERTIVENESS

Requiring courage, respect, and skill, Respectful Confrontation takes the game of communication to its highest level. When you can see each encounter with the freshness and playfulness of a game, or a martial arts sparring match, all your interactions take on a light, peaceful, and creative tone—no matter how superficial or intense the topic of conversation. When you confront another with the intention to grow and deepen relationship, and you open to the unknown, an excitement and joy emerges.

———(?)

- *What is your relationship with games, sports, and competition? Some of us enjoy games; some of us don't. Some of us play fairly; some of us cheat. Some of us enjoy the sport and the thrill of risk-taking while some of us don't even get in the game or are sore losers. Some of us play so that everyone wins and benefits from the experience while some of us manipulate the rules for our own selfish gains and to defeat others.*

- *Which resonates with you? Determine how well you play, how much risk you take, how safe you play or if you even play at all.*
- *How do you relate to others?*
- *How do you approach difficult conversations?*
- *Are you good with small talk?*
- *Are you comfortable speaking your truth?*
- *Are you good with hearing the truth of another even if you get some difficult feedback?*
- *Can you easily express what you need or what you are feeling?*
- *Are you the one who brings up the difficult topics that need to be discussed?*
- *Do you put a lot of energy into keeping the peace even if it means lying or sacrificing your own needs?*

Your responses to these questions will give you an idea of how willing you are to confront and take the risk of speaking your truth. In order to deepen relationship and empower all involved, you always run the risk that something will be gained and something will be lost. Generally speaking, the reasons to confront are to illuminate an unspoken truth, or review some behaviors or patterns that need to be acknowledged or changed. To get the discussion going, someone has to start. This requires courage.

In martial arts, two opponents come to the mat ready for competition. They stand opposite one another in a powerful confrontation—open and vulnerable. Anything is possible; each is ready to use her power and skills to stay in the game until the end—with respect and honor, excited to be challenged, and hoping for a worthy opponent. And there they are—standing and waiting, waiting and standing. The clock ticks away. No one is moving. Yes they are centered; yes they have a strong contact and connection. They are grounded and focused. There they stand, waiting.

What is missing? Neither one of them dares to assert and make the first move and step out into the unknown. Even though both seem to be safe, balanced, and centered, the lack of assertion has led to vagueness, dispersing and wasting of energy, distraction, and paralysis.

Do you recognize this pattern in your interactions and communication with others? How often have you decided to confront another, but at the last moment, stepped aside and pulled back—frozen and waiting for the other to take the initiative? *Every time you avoid speaking your truth and addressing an important issue, you move one step closer to conflict and misunderstanding.*

Assertiveness, and the Practice of Respectful Offense, is the next phase in Respectful Confrontation. When you assert, you step into unknown territory where you are not sure of what the outcome will be. To confront is like being a pioneer. You are an advocate for growth, learning, change, intimacy, and creative collaboration, and that requires you to step out of the realm of the familiar. The Respectful Confronter understands that to maintain good health and balance, personally and in relationship with others and society, things have to change and grow. Trying to avoid change leads to unhealthy, conflicted situations.

Like in a martial arts match, it is essential that you take the first step in order to get the interaction started. You take a risk and muster up the courage to connect, to speak your truth, and dare to hear the truth of others. Something is sacrificed; something is gained. The game begins.

ASSERTIVENESS VS. AGGRESSION

When you assert, you feel the thrill of taking a risk, taking yourself out of your own safe space, and moving into the space of another. You have started the dance of life. You are now in the natural flow and rhythm of the universe. You feel alive.

When your intention is to deepen relationship and empower all involved, you invite the other to step into her power. You give the person permission to take a risk, to step out of her space into your space, and feel the thrill of asserting. *By giving her space to assert, you have helped to empower her.*

This is a higher view of assertiveness and power. You don't assert to conquer and beat others down, but to call others to their highest empowerment. When you get into a place of no judgment and risk-taking, you feel a sensation flow through you that is vital, playful, open, free, and creative. This is what power feels like! If you experience power as heavy, brute-like, violent, and destructive, then you are misusing power.

To be assertive is tricky because you are forced to step out of your own personal space and move into the space of another to have an impact. There may be fear, but the Respectful Confronter overcomes the fear and perseveres. This is true courage. Being courageous doesn't mean that you are always free of fear; it means you can stand openhearted in the face of fear, move forward, and still maintain your centeredness and presence. Maya Angelou, award-winning American poet, said, "One isn't necessarily born with courage, but one is born with potential. Without courage, we cannot practice any other virtue with consistency. We can't be kind, true, merciful, generous or honest."

You are more visible and open to criticism when you begin to assert yourself. You are more influential and have a larger impact. This can be intimidating to others and can bring you more responsibility. The more you assert, the more you run the risk that you will overpower others, trigger their insecurities or they may perceive your assertive impulses as aggression. Others may want to pull you down. Yet, when you take this risk, you have "upped the ante" on your interactions, leading to more vital, immediate confrontations. You are now in the game to win! To win for you and for others. How exciting!

Many of us avoid asserting ourselves because we hold on to an old belief that assertiveness and aggression are the same. This is another one of those paradigms that we need to shift in order to move into a more honorable, respectful way of engaging with others. Just like confrontation and conflict, assertiveness and aggression are not the same. And once again, the strongest factor that makes them different is the motivation. Let's take a closer look at both.

Many of us were taught that to assert means to harm, to conquer, and to disempower. Both men and women have adapted this old-fashioned image of an assertive person as a way of making it in the world. This "win at all costs" view of assertiveness and power benefits a small few and has had devastating consequences on the masses and the planet. Former U.S. president Ronald Reagan said, "History teaches that war begins when governments believe the price of aggression is cheap."

If you didn't want to function in this way, and if you thought that assertiveness and aggression were the same thing, you probably taught yourself to hold back speaking your truth and keep your full power to yourself. If you valued compassion and cooperation, you may have sacrificed your own needs. Because you assumed the results would be devastating, you may have lied to yourself and others by not speaking your truth.

You can change this! Our future depends on the compassionate ones, the caregivers, the peacemakers, and the ones who advocate cooperation and respect to step up and dare to assert a new way of using power. U.S. congressman Barney Frank said, "Reality is the enemy of prejudice."

Webster's dictionary defines ASSERTIVE in the following way:

As·ser·tive

1   disposed to or characterized by bold or confident **assertion** <an *assertive* leader>

2   having a strong or distinctive flavor or aroma <*assertive* wines>

Notice the lack of malice and the emphasis on strength and confidence.

And this is how Webster's Dictionary defines AGGRESSIVE:

Ag·gres·sive

1   a: tending toward or exhibiting **aggression** <*aggressive* behavior>
     b: marked by combative readiness <an *aggressive* fighter>

2   a: marked by obtrusive energy
     b: marked by driving forceful energy or initiative: enterprising <an *aggressive* salesman>

Here you see an emphasis on combat and an invasive, unwelcome quality.

I define ASSERTIVENESS as:

any behavior, action, remark, gesture or facial expression that impacts another with the goal to empower the other, and/or is received in a positive way.

At its simplest, for something to be considered ASSERTIVE, it must have two factors:

1   *it must be an action, statement, gesture or even a lack of these*
2   *it must have somehow entered the personal space of another and have a beneficial effect on that person*

When you *assert* yourself, you step out of your comfort zone to speak your truth, affect positive change, accomplish your goals or connect with others. In order to be sure that your assertive action is a Respectful Confrontation and will not lead to conflict and possible aggression, you need to check the motivation of your action. The goal of your action must be to create collaboration, connection, deepening of relationship, and the empowerment of all involved.

I define AGGRESSION as:

any behavior, action, remark, gesture or facial expression that impacts another with the goal to disempower the other, and/or is received in a harmful, threatening way.

At its simplest, for something to be considered AGGRESSIVE, it must have two factors:

1   *it must be an action, statement, gesture or even a lack of these*
2   *it must somehow enter the personal space of another and have an adverse effect on that person*

Funny. When you think about the definition of assertiveness, it looks almost the same! Both start with some kind of action, gesture or statement that moves out of your personal space, moves into the personal space of someone else, and has some kind of effect on those around you. This is why we often confuse assertiveness with aggression. They are almost identical.

However, now we see the difference. An assertive act has a positive effect on the other; an aggressive act disempowers the other. *No matter what you do or what your motivation is, it all comes down to how the other feels!* You have asserted yourself when the other feels that your action has had a positive effect on them. If your action causes her to feel pain, fear or anything else that may disempower her, then what you have done can be considered aggressive.

This shows how fragile confrontation is and how sensitive your actions and words can be. The only way to be sure of how you are impacting the other is to stay engaged, be mindful of your actions and words, and *check in with the other to see how your message was received.* Because this seems tedious and time-consuming, we tend to pull back, to be timid, and avoid moving into others' space for fear of hurting them. This is a shame. We may succeed in avoiding fights and keeping the peace, but we also don't speak up for ourselves and end up living an unfulfilled life.

Then there are those who go the other way. They are people who think that as long as they get their needs met and push their personal agenda, they have no problem stepping out of their personal space and into the personal space of others. They don't care if they hurt or bully others or are overbearing. They are the ones who usually say, "Oh, stop being so sensitive" when you try to express your feelings and needs, and confront them with their behavior. They may succeed in the short term, but they aren't aware of how much resentment is building up that will eventually lead to conflict and strife for all involved. Brute force is no longer working as we move into an "age of relationship" where we see how interdependent individuals and nations are.

The solution to finding balance between these two extremes is practicing presence, centeredness, true power, openhearted engagement, and clear communication. The more mindful you are of your actions and asserting your feelings and needs instead of using subversive ways to get what you want, the better chance you have of avoiding conflict and aggression and accomplishing your goals.

When you assert, it is impossible to know in advance how the other is going to react, or how you are going to respond in the heat of the moment. As long as you know that your motivation is to deepen relationship and to empower both of you, you can assert yourself with confidence.

If for some reason the other still feels like you are being aggressive and not assertive, it is your obligation get to the cause of the breakdown in communication and do what is necessary to get back to openness and connection. This is the dance of giving and receiving, and of strength and flexibility.

⑦

- *What is your relationship with assertiveness?*
- *Do you find it easy or difficult?*
- *Are you afraid of it or do you assert with ease?*
- *Do you express your needs and feelings?*
- *Do you put forth ideas at work?*
- *Do you dare to speak your truth even if it means rocking the boat?*
- *Do you express your creativity?*
- *Do you step up as a leader in areas where you excel?*
- *Do you take action to help and support others?*
- *Are you comfortable with introducing yourself to others?*
- *Do you dare to stand out and make a mark on the world?*
- *Are you open to having an impact on others and your surroundings?*

These are essential questions to ask if you are committed to finding personal freedom, fulfillment, and being a positive influence on others. As you develop the skills of Respectful Confrontation, you will gain confidence in asserting yourself with courage, respect, and understanding. When you know that speaking your truth won't lead to aggression, violence or unfair consequences to others, then you will truly assert yourself, find fulfillment, share the full capacity of your wisdom and gifts, and have a strong, positive impact on the world.

So overcome your fears and insecurities, step out of your personal space, and assert your needs, your feelings, your viewpoints, and your desires. Contemplate the differences between assertiveness and aggression. Know that when you are in your *true power* that you aren't destructive or hurtful. You can speak your truth, even when someone else begins to get reactive, because you have the skills and wisdom to stay centered and connected, grounded and focused in an openhearted way.

"My boss asked me to do a last minute assignment. Usually I would do it, which meant little sleep, less time with my kids, and running myself down. This time I tried it differently. I sent an email to him on Monday, saying I couldn't get the project done when he wanted me to and I suggested an alternate date that worked for me. He replied, 'I can live with that, thanks.' It worked beautifully."

"

PERSONAL SPACE

To acknowledge your boundaries and personal space, and that of another, is a necessary tool when asserting yourself. What is the importance of establishing your personal space? What does it mean to step out of your own personal space? What happens when you step into someone else's personal space?

The more clarity you have about your own personal space, the more secure you feel about yourself and the world. This sense of security will allow you to engage easier with others with confidence and presence. You have more acceptance of what you encounter. It is empowering to affirm your right to your own space, and it is liberating and healing to set your boundaries and choose your own level of safety. To know that it is *your* choice whether someone enters your personal space or not might be a new concept for you.

Most of us suffer from a wounded view of self and personal space because on some level we have had our boundaries ignored or we managed to betray our own boundaries. If you have a history of abuse as a child, you were probably given the message that you didn't have the right to your own space; you may have had to sacrifice your personal safety and needs to the whims of others. As children, we may not have been able to protect ourselves or claim and assert our boundaries; but as an adult, you can determine who has the right and privilege to get close to you. You get to determine how deep and intimate you choose to be with others. At the same time, you respect the boundaries of others, understanding that to be allowed to enter someone's personal space is an honor and a responsibility that requires trust and accountability.

This is essential in the process of Respectful Confrontation; *how you move into someone's space, and whether you are invited, will determine if your action is assertiveness or aggression.* Many misunderstandings arise from a lack of clarity with establishing healthy boundaries. Observe yourself and others in public situations.

- *Do you let people enter your space too easily or not enough?*
- *Do you betray your own boundaries in order to keep the peace?*
- *How does your behavior influence others?*
- *Do you push into other people's space without even knowing you are doing it?*
- *Are you too timid to connect with others or influence those around you?*

This is how you can determine how much of what you do and what you don't do may contribute to the growth and deepening of relationship or to disempowerment and separation. The more honest you can be without judging yourself and others, the quicker you can make adjustments to find greater harmony with yourself and your environment. This has a profound and healing effect. The following exercise will help you to have a concrete experience of your personal space.

MASTERING RESPECTFUL CONFRONTATION

E X E R C I S E
PERSONAL SPACE

**BEFORE YOU START THIS EXERCISE, REVIEW
"HOW TO USE THIS BOOK" ON PAGE 23**

PRELIMINARY STEPS

(see APPENDIX ONE on page 281 for details)

- ▷ **Choose a good time and location**
- ▷ **Start with the basic standing pose**
- ▷ **Bring your attention to your center**
- ▷ **Place all of your attention on your breath**

MAIN STEPS

- ▸ **Explore the immediate space around you**

Stretch your arms out and see how far they reach. This is approximately the size of your personal space. Explore this space in great detail. Use your hands to determine the boundary of your space: in front of you, behind you, above and below, left and right. Make this space as real as you can. This boundary you are creating distinguishes your personal space from the rest of the world.

▶ **Explore the area inside of the boundaries of your personal space**
Smell it, feel it, maybe you hear a specific sound, maybe you see colors, maybe you see the boundary of your space taking on a certain material, like glass, paper or stone. Don't try to think too much while doing this. Notice which thoughts, images, and feelings arise. These impulses are coming from a more authentic place than your intellectual interpretation of this. Trust these impulses.

▶ **Imagine that your personal space is completely sealed off**
Look at the space inside of the boundary and take a look at everything else outside of it. See and feel a difference between the two. Maybe the temperature is different, the colors, the light. Sealing off your space doesn't mean that others can't enter. It simply means that you are clear about the moment when someone moves into your space.

▶ **Feel the comfort and safety within your personal space**
As you establish the space inside your boundary and the space outside, say to yourself that the space inside is always safe. It is calm, comforting, and pleasant to be in. It is like being "home". Assure yourself that as long as no one comes into your personal space you are safe; you take a risk letting someone enter your "safe zone".

Feel that safety and comfort. See and feel yourself standing in the middle of your personal space. Close your eyes and take a few minutes to stand there in silence and notice what feelings and thoughts come up. Keep breathing steadily, allowing any emotions to flow.

▶ **Open your eyes again and look out at the world around you**

Finish the exercise with a few minutes of observing yourself in your surroundings. This is the same world you have always looked at, but try to see it with a new perspective from inside your personal space. You are still in relationship with the world and all that you encounter, but with an added awareness. Feel how much space you take up. Dare to fill your space, let yourself be on this planet. *You have the right to this space!* Observe how it feels to engage with the world and also know that your space is only occupied by you. And observe how it feels to think that you are safe as long as no one comes into your space. Allow any feelings, thoughts or sensations to flow until you are done with the exercise.

CLOSING STEPS

(see APPENDIX ONE on page 283 for details)

▷ **Shake out and stretch your legs**

▷ **Make notes on what you have discovered**

RECOMMENDED SCHEDULE

It should take you about fifteen to thirty minutes to make your personal space concrete. If you practice this regularly you will build up a habit of seeing and feeling your boundaries with no effort, increasing self-confidence and personal freedom. *Since this exercise is the foundation for all of the other exercises in the sections The Practice of Respectful Offense and The Practice of Respectful Defense, practice it often.*

 TIPS

When you have a good sense of your own personal space, try doing this exercise in different environments, like in nature or at work, and also when you are around other people. Notice if you are still able to hold onto a sense of your boundaries. How close do you let others get to you? How courageous are you to move into someone else's space without being aggressive? Tell others that you are practicing this exercise or keep it to yourself.

You may decide to do this exercise with someone who is willing to practice and explore with you and is willing to give you honest feedback. It is ideal to practice with someone, or a group of people, who are also reading this book and studying the practices. This will help you gain more sensitivity in recognizing the personal space of others in a controlled setting.

"Confront my mother? No way! She would either start yelling, or go quiet and get all pitiful. No one in the family has been able to deal with that. Even though I don't think I could really confront her yet, I am able to at least say what is true for me. I don't criticize, but share what I am feeling. This is having a positive effect on all of us, without her feeling threatened."

RESPECTFUL OFFENSE: GIVING FEEDBACK

After a detailed exploration of the preparatory steps, we will now examine what a confrontation looks like. *The goal of Respectful Confrontation is to speak your truth and to bring to light unspoken issues and behaviors that are influencing you and the other. The same is also true for confronting aspects within yourself.*

When things are not brought out into the light, miscommunication and assumptions about one another create suspicion, resentment, and unconscious wounding. These unspoken patterns, feelings, and needs eat away at the heart connection, causing the breakdown of relationship, separation, and lack of growth.

Because of *fear, embarrassment, addictions, resistance to being vulnerable, and an aversion to being uncomfortable,* we don't express what needs to be spoken to deepen relationship and foster growth. The role of confrontation is to cut through all these obstacles and get us back into, or deepen, the openhearted connection.

With *presence, centeredness, and openhearted engagement*, the next step is to take the initiative and assert your truth. In order to be successful with his offensive moves, a martial artist needs a clear structure and strategy for attack. Random kicks and punches might have some effect, but he will most likely get knocked down or wear himself out. To successfully use Respectful Offense in your confrontation, a clear structure and approach will guarantee better results in achieving your goal.

Here is a useful breakdown of how to present your truth when confronting yourself or others. Of course, you can't expect that every time you use this tool that you will succeed. You will never know how open the other will be to cooperating or if the person will go into reactive behavior. But with this structured approach to confrontation, *what you can be sure of is that you have done your best to effectively communicate your feelings, needs, and truth.*

The fewer distractions and the better prepared you are, the more likely you will stay on target and achieve your goal. A healthy confrontation should be done when both individuals are calm and not caught up in disturbing emotions. A time should be chosen when both have the time to talk and in an environment that is calm and not distracting.

You may be ready for a deep, vulnerable discussion but the other person may not. Even though he may have agreed to have this conversation with you, he will most likely find ways to distract you from getting to the truth of the matter. This tendency to avoid the uncomfortable conversations is a familiar unconscious pattern we all have.

I have shared this exercise with many people in my workshops and seminars, and *experience has shown that it is important to include all the steps in this process.* This may seem tedious, but if you miss one or a number of the steps, you run the risk of getting sidetracked by the other, ending up in a conflict, or having an abrupt, unsatisfying end to the conversation. When this happens, you will probably spend more time later picking up the pieces of the failed conversation. So, take the time now to include all of the following steps.

NINE STEPS OF RESPECTFUL OFFENSE

(1) **PREPARE**

Come with specific facts and examples to back up your truth concerning the issues that you want to confront. Refer to real situations, not abstract ideas or opinions. Be tangible and you will get the other to see your point.

Having clear examples will help if the other denies what you are asserting. Let's use the example of your partner repeatedly not doing the dishes after she agreed to do them. If you say that she hasn't done the dishes and she says that she did, then you need to come up with dates and times to back up your claim. Also, preparation will give the impression to the other that you are serious about this issue and the relationship. This can only have a positive effect.

Another way to prepare is to write down beforehand what you want to say and actually rehearse it out loud. Think about how the other may get defensive or deny what you are claiming. Think about what familiar reactive behavior and strategies she may use to distract and derail you from getting to the truth. Formulate in advance your strategies of how to address this without getting thrown.

Clarify how much time will be needed, so there is no misunderstanding. You may assume that you have thirty minutes for this confrontation, but because it is not clear how urgent this is to you, the other may only allow about ten minutes.

(2) MAKE CONTACT

Now that you are prepared, it is time to approach the other, either in a spontaneous encounter or at a chosen date and time. When you meet with her, get present, centered, open to your true power, and establish your personal space as well as hers. This doesn't have to take long. If you have already practiced these tools often, you can do all of this in less than a minute. Review the exercises in The Practice of Developing the Respectful Self as well as the exercise "Personal Space" on page 183.

Make contact with the other person. Do whatever you need to do to get connected in an easy, flowing way, and with respect and understanding. Make eye contact; connect from your center. Feel how much openhearted connection there is. Be sure to breathe. You may need some small talk to get the two of you more connected and grounded. Review the exercises in The Practice of Respectful Engagement.

The other doesn't have to know these techniques to make contact with you. If you make the effort to connect, she will find a way to connect with you. *If possible, turn off your phones and any other electronic devices!*

(3) INTRODUCE THE TOPIC

When you feel that there is a good connection, bring up the issue that needs to be confronted *and then be silent.* Give the other a chance to go through the process of understanding what the subject is about and what the consequences may be. She will probably go through dozens of emotions and thoughts before she reacts.

When she realizes how important this discussion will be, she may get uncomfortable (a good sign). If she feels threatened, she will already be strategizing ways to get out of facing the truth of this issue. Give her time to go through all these feelings and reactions.

④ **SHARE WHAT YOU HAVE NOTICED ABOUT THE BEHAVIOR IN QUESTION**

After you have given her a moment to understand what you want to address, now you can bring up the specific behavior that she is doing that you want to confront. Go slow. Give her time to see the situation from your perspective.

All you can express is how *you* see the situation. This doesn't mean that you are right. You are simply expressing *your* truth. Simply present the situation from your perspective and what you have observed. Do not present it in a way that sounds like you are condemning, judging or accusing. That will make her defensive and cause her to shut down.

The only thing you can really confront people on is their behavior—something that they are doing, saying, thinking, or not doing. There is a big difference between bringing up someone's behavior and criticizing the person. Criticizing the person always leads to conflict.

You can't change a person. However, you can influence a person by making them aware of their behavior. Contemplate this concept. People don't change; behavior can change. When behavior changes, you transform. The only thing you can influence is your behavior and the behavior of others in order to hopefully help yourself and others. Then the relationship can transform for the better. Well-known Chinese thinker and philosopher Confucius said, "Men's natures are alike, it is their habits that carry them far apart."

For instance, you can confront someone for the behavior of not doing the dishes when she said she would. You won't get anywhere if you attack her character and you call her a slob.

⑤ EXPRESS HOW THE BEHAVIOR AFFECTS YOU

At this point in your confrontation, express to the other how her behavior affects you. This can be a feeling, a state of being, or an unmet need. If the behavior of the other is causing deepening of relationship and loving feelings, let them know. If their behavior is causing separation and the disempowerment of you or others, express that.

This is the most critical point in the Practice of Respectful Offense. This is what will make or break your confrontation and ensure a successful outcome. *In fact, this step is so crucial, that it has the potential to transform you and all of your relationships.*

You may say, "when you don't do the dishes when you say you will, I come home from work nervous and anxious (feeling) because I can't be sure if I will be able to cook. It causes me a lot of stress." Or you may say, "Not doing the dishes when you say you will leaves me with the feeling that you don't respect me" (state of being). Or, "Because you don't do the dishes when you say you will, I feel unsure of how reliable you are in honoring your commitments. It starts with the dishes; where will it go from there? I don't feel secure (unmet need) in our commitment to each other."

The wise person knows that it's never really about the dishes. If you only address the problem of the dishes, then nothing will be solved. It will remain on the level of "I want you to do..." This won't go anywhere. You get to the real issues when you express needs and feelings, so that growth and resolution can happen.

To have the courage to speak about how someone's behavior affects you means you are really speaking *your* truth. You are making yourself vulnerable and making it difficult for the other to deflect. When you clearly help her to see that her behavior is having a deeper, emotional effect on you, and if she is a rational person who has something invested in this relationship, she will yield and choose to collaborate and seek out solutions. Your assertive tactics have brought her to a point where she will probably comply. If she truly understands that her behavior is making you feel insecure, disrespected, and nervous and she chooses to continue that behavior, then it may be time for you to question the integrity of the relationship.

It is essential to have a fluency in the language of feelings and needs. Be specific and zero in precisely on how the behavior of the other is affecting you. Create your own list of feelings and needs. If you need some help to understand exactly what this is, take a look at Developing the Vocabulary of Feelings and Needs on page 151.

In a challenging confrontation, it is important to get to this step as quickly as you can. By leaving this step out, you end up criticizing the other and judging them. The information you present comes across as patronizing—as if you think you are better and as if you are accusing the other of being bad. The natural reaction of the other is to defend and get into the cycle of "I am right. You are wrong." This usually leads to conflict, separation, and the breakdown of the openhearted connection.

Once you have asserted your truth, stay silent and let the other take it all in. Stay centered and alert for her next move. Using the Four Pillars of True Power will help you stay grounded, focused, and in your power. Since the other probably won't want to hear this truth, she will come up with ways to distract you, like excuses, evasive behavior, and denial to name a few. You will have to dance skillfully with all her reactive behavior and aggressive strategies in order to persevere and move closer to your goal. We will explore in detail successful ways to address this reactive behavior in The Practice of Respectful Defense.

⑥ IDENTIFY YOUR NEED

Before you seek out solutions and resolution, or reinforce the other's positive behavior, speak clearly about what you need and desire. The reason you are confronting the other is to illuminate how her behavior is affecting you. If it is a positive effect, appreciate her and acknowledge the need that *is* being met. If her behavior is causing you to feel frustrated, to close your heart or distance yourself from the other, then identify what you would need to get back into openhearted connection.

Be specific. It is easier to find solutions when you can clearly express a need like "I would like more reassurance. I need clarity in our agreements." Again, check the list of needs in Developing the Vocabulary of Feelings and Needs on page 157 to get a clear idea of what a need is. Remember, your need is an internal signal within *you, not something outside of yourself.* If you start your sentence with, " I need *you* to...," you are not expressing your need; you are disguising your *want* or *thought* with the word *need*.

This is also the moment to hear from the other what she needs to make this situation amenable for both of you.

⑦ COME UP WITH SOLUTIONS. MENTION DESIRED BEHAVIOR

Now that you have identified what you both need, you begin the process of negotiating and searching for solutions. This is a time of listening and being generous to yourself and the other, where growth, empowerment, and deepening can happen. Use collaboration and openhearted creativity. Make some clear agreements and be specific in expressing the desired behavior. If you keep it vague, then you run the risk that the same pattern will be repeated.

Give suggestions for what can be done to ensure that your needs are met. Let the other come with ideas and listen to what challenges her. Maybe she has a problem that she hasn't felt courageous enough to share with you. There may be legitimate reasons why she is not getting to the dishes. You may find out that she is overstressed at work because of new management and she actually needs your support at the moment. *This is how asserting your truth encourages others to do the same and how you both benefit from the confrontation.* Stay committed to getting your needs met and also listen with understanding and generosity.

(8) SUM UP AND AGREE ON HOW YOU WILL FOLLOW UP

Check in with how you both are feeling and if you both have been heard by the other. Sum up what you have discussed and then set up a time to check in again and evaluate how this new arrangement is going. When you look back at past attempts to confront others, you may see that things changed for the better for a few days but then went back to the old ways. This is common.

It takes a long time to change habits. If we all were able to change immediately, we wouldn't have the problems, personal or global, that we have. Be generous, compassionate, and especially patient. You may need to confront this issue many times before you see lasting change.

Feel comforted in knowing that if things are moving in the right direction, it won't be as challenging the next time if you have to confront this issue again.

⑨ BRING THE CONFRONTATION TO A CLOSE

You have taken special care to make contact and stay engaged through all the twists and turns of this confrontation. The other has shown the same level of involvement and desire to collaborate towards a solution. This is a good moment to acknowledge and honor this. Usually, at the end of a match, regardless of who wins or loses, the martial artist will face his opponent one last time and bow, showing his honor and respect for the other's skill and display of power.

Use any gesture that will show your respect and appreciation, like a hug, handshake or a verbal acknowledgement. Now you can get on with the rest of your day.

....

These are the nine steps to effectively give feedback and confront in a respectful, empowered way. When you master this tool, you have mastered the Practice of Respectful Offense. This approach to communicating with yourself and others will transform you and your relationships.

If you feel these confrontations are not working and moving towards growth, then first take a look at how effective and specific you are in your communication. You may think that you are confronting with an open heart and understanding, but in actuality you may be overdoing it and bullying the other. You may be using brute force to get your way, as opposed to coming from a place of vulnerability, respect, and generosity where the needs of the other are also honored and met.

If you are confronting in a healthy way and you still notice that the two of you are drifting, then the truth may be emerging that the relationship is nearing its end. This won't always happen when you confront, but it is also a possibility that many of us avoid. If the goal is ultimately the empowerment of all involved and getting to the truth, then what may be revealed is that the best solution for the two of you is to separate. If this conclusion comes from Respectful Confrontation, then the process of parting will come from a mutual, loving, and openhearted place and not from resentment, conflict, and the disempowerment of the other.

Chances are, however, you and the other will grow deeper in your connection. *Every confrontation is an affirmation of your love, respect, and commitment.* When you confront, you are saying that you are willing to go through the discomfort to find the deeper beauty of what you are building with each other. You become two courageous beings willing to stand face-to-face in openhearted vulnerability to reveal your true power.

Speaking to the other about what you are feeling and needing opens you up to vulnerability which is the very thing that causes the heart to open and ignites the desire to find solutions. I see it over and over again with clients, with students, and with myself; even though we know that expressing our feelings and needs is essential, we still find it challenging to do.

The three key points to a successful confrontation are:
- *Clearly talk about the other's behavior, not judge the person*
- *Be specific about how their behavior is impacting you (the feeling, state of being, unmet need)*
- *State clearly what you need*

Giving feedback is the number one offensive tool of Respectful Confrontation. Like all the tools in this book, this too requires practice. For many of us, we may start with good intentions, but in the heat of the moment we feel the reactive behavior of the other and our attempt to be assertive fails. We somehow fall back into old patterns of accusations, blame, and mixed messages that result in more confusion and misunderstanding. This is the moment when you will feel how much courage is needed to persevere and speak your truth, and the importance of thorough preparation. The more you repeat this process with exercises and in a safe, controlled environment, the easier it will be to follow through and succeed in a real situation.

Here is a useful exercise to help you figure out and structure the things that you will say when you confront both yourself and people in your life. It may feel strange to write out and actually recite in advance the things you would like to say to others, but the more prepared you are, the more likely you will stay centered and follow through. This is similar to a martial artist spending hours punching and kicking until it becomes second nature. A pianist is not going to perform a new piece until she feels confident that she knows the music inside and out.

Don't limit your confrontations to just negative issues. Speaking your truth about your appreciation of others is another way to deepen relationship, bring you and others closer together, and empower all involved. However, we will focus here on the more challenging confrontations because they tend to be hardest to do.

You may also find that in order to feel more empowered, and experience personal freedom and fulfillment, you must confront aspects of yourself that are holding you back—like a habit, belief system, fear, or addiction. Feel free to include them in this exercise.

OUTLINING YOUR CONFRONTATIONS

**BEFORE YOU START THIS EXERCISE, REVIEW
"HOW TO USE THIS BOOK" ON PAGE 23**

PRELIMINARY STEPS

(see APPENDIX ONE on page 281 for details)

▷ **Choose a good time and location**

▷ **Start with the basic sitting pose**

▷ **Bring your attention to your center**

▷ **Place all of your attention on your breath**

MAIN STEPS

▸ **Get some paper or a journal and a pen**

If you enjoy drawing, you may want to get pens of different colors.

▸ **Think of all the people (or aspects of yourself) that you feel you need to confront.**

Who do you feel that you have issues with? Who do you feel that you have closed your heart to that you would like to find a way to open it up again? Who is causing you to feel disempowered or with whom do you feel you can't fully be yourself? Who would you like to appreciate?

Think about certain character traits within yourself that you feel are holding you back and keeping you from living your true potential and finding personal freedom and fulfillment. This could be a habit, belief system, fear or an addiction. Here are some examples: *a belief that you will always struggle financially, being cynical, being chronically late, living in a messy home.*

This step may trigger feelings and emotions. Allow them to flow. Try not to judge yourself or the other for the behaviors that need to be confronted. Approach this exercise with compassion and understanding.

▸ **Make a list of these people and personal character traits**

In this beginning phase, give yourself the space to write without censuring. Let your thoughts flow. Write from your heart. Nobody needs to see this. You can sort your notes later.

▸ **Write the following headlines across the top of another page:**

NAME | BEHAVIOR | EFFECT | NEED | DESIRED BEHAVIOR | FOLLOW UP

▸ **Sort out your notes by filling in the information for each confrontation under the headlines above.**

Under **NAME**, write the name of the person or character trait that you would like to confront.

Under **BEHAVIOR**, put into a few words the behavior that is causing you stress or closing your heart. It is important to remember that you are only referring to the behavior, not the person. You can't change a person, but you can influence behavior.

Under **EFFECT**, write down in a clear way how this behavior is influencing you. This will be a feeling, an emotion, a state of being, an unhealthy pattern or an unmet need.

Under **NEED**, clearly put into words the thing that you are missing, and therefore desire having. According to you, if this unmet need could be honored, then this would shift the situation from one that feels disempowering to one that is open, creative, and from the heart. What you need is unique to you. Some examples are: *to be seen, security, belonging, collaboration.*

Write down the **DESIRED BEHAVIOR**. Now that you have identified the need that you are hoping to get fulfilled, what could the other do to ensure that this need is met? This creates the opening with the other to come up with creative solutions in a way that should work for both of you. This allows for the two of you to collaborate.

Write down a proposed **FOLLOW UP**. Finally, make sure you come up with a clear way to check up on the progress of this new agreement. Write down a clear system to see if both of you are following through with your commitments. This could be something like, "let's talk again in two weeks to follow up."

▸ **Repeat this process with all the people and personal character traits on your list.**

Take as much time as you want. Revise. Be honest and clear.

▸ **Practice on your own what you would say, based on the notes you made.**

Talk out loud with yourself, or ask a trusted friend to join you and practice with them. If you do this on your own, just keep repeating your statements over and over again.

If you ask a friend to help out, they don't need to say anything, just listen. You could ask for feedback once you have finished the process.

Ask them how your confrontation affected them. Were you

clear? Assertive? Too timid? Too aggressive? Ask them if they have any suggestions on how you can speak your truth with confidence and clarity, and from a place of understanding and compassion.

CLOSING STEPS
(see APPENDIX ONE on page 283 for details)
▷ **Shake out and stretch your legs**
▷ **Make notes on what you have discovered**

RECOMMENDED SCHEDULE
Recite the same scenarios over and over until you feel like the words flow easily.

 TIPS

You have not arrived yet at the stage of actually confronting the people and personal character traits on your list. You are just practicing your offensive moves—like rehearsing for a play—so that when you actually do have to confront, you will have the confidence that you can communicate in a clear and powerful way, even if the other starts getting emotional, evasive or aggressive. Recite your scenarios until they become second nature and part of your "muscle memory".

Your list and approach for your situations would probably look different if someone else were to do the same. How you are *affected*, and what you *need*, will be different as well as the *solutions* you come up with. This is the power of diversity and creativity and why there is not one answer to our problems.

As mentioned before, there is no way to know how the other will react and what the outcome will be. This is why you must be as prepared as possible to ensure that, no matter how the discussion goes, you can say you did your best. Having a clear and powerful offensive strategy will make it easier for you to navigate the unconscious reactions, emotions, and aggression of the other. We are now ready to explore The Practice of Respectful Defense.

EXAMPLE OF
RESPECTFUL OFFENSE
OUTLINING YOUR CONFRONTATION

Jack and Nina are partners and live together. Both had an agreement that Nina would take on the chore of doing the dishes. For the last three weeks, Nina has not done the dishes. Before Jack confronts Nina, he would prepare his list and recite it many times.

Here is what his list could look like:

NAME	Nina
BEHAVIOR	not do the dishes
EFFECT	not feel comfortable in home, not feel respected, insecure because Nina is not honoring agreements, fear that she may not honor other commitments
NEED	security that the commitments we make are valid and respected
DESIRED BEHAVIOR	follow through with commitments, make new agreements that we both feel we can follow through with, revisit agreement about dishes and chores
FOLLOW UP	evaluate in two weeks how it's going

Here is an example of how Jack can practice saying this out loud:

"Nina, I want to talk about the fact that you are not doing the dishes. Because you are not following through with our agreement, I feel disrespected, and I am feeling unsure of you following through with your commitments. I would like to feel secure in our commitment to one another. So, what I need is the assurance that when we make agreements, you will make an effort to follow through, or let me know that you acknowledge our agreement but you are not able to honor it right now. So, I would like to revisit our agreement about you doing the dishes and see if we can come up with something that we both feel good about. Either you do the dishes as we agreed, or maybe we need to switch chores for a while. With this new agreement, I'd like to connect and see how it is going in two weeks."

BEN'S STORY

During the past year, I have been faced with a very stressful work situation. As a social worker in a non-profit, I came to understand that there has been some serious mismanagement within our agency, resulting in clients not receiving adequate services and staff feeling fearful of retaliation if they spoke up.

In past situations, when I have felt that social injustice was occurring, I tended to get very angry and not be able to channel my energies very well. Instead, I would vent my anger in a very non-productive way and leave the setting feeling dissatisfied and frustrated. Sometimes I would bottle it up inside of me and not say anything at all. Although I felt confident that shining the light on some of the social injustices was the right thing to do, I too was worried that my job could be at risk.

As a result of attending Respectful Confrontation, I realized how important it was to speak my truth in a respectful manner. When I communicated with the board, I used some of my new tools, like the "Four Pillars of True Power". This helped me to deliver a clear message and not get derailed when I was met with resistance. I made sure to speak about feelings and needs and not make demands that would threaten. The more I spoke out, the more I realized that taking a non-aggressive stance, yet still confronting the wrongdoing, was in itself a victory.

The people that pulled me aside and tried to intimidate me had very little power over me, because the tools of Respectful Confrontation gave me the skills and courage I needed to follow through.

Since first speaking out, there have been some positive changes. Our board meetings are now open to the public for the first time in twenty-seven years. The board members finally did a formal performance evaluation of our Executive Director, which led to her being rightfully fired. They also began a major restructuring of the agency, which will benefit an entire community that relies on our agency.

I can't believe how effective I was. The tools of Respectful Confrontation supported me in speaking my truth and benefiting many people.

KEY POINTS

ASSERTIVENESS .... ✓

PERSONAL SPACE .... ✓

NINE STEPS OF RESPECTFUL OFFENSE .... ✓

GIVING FEEDBACK .... ✓

TOPICS FOR CONTEMPLATION OR JOURNALING

- *What is your relationship with games, sports, and competition?*
- *How do you relate to others? What is your relationship with asserting?*
- *Are you comfortable with speaking your truth? Are you comfortable with hearing the truth of others?*
- *What does courage mean to you?*
- *How are assertiveness and aggression similar and different to you?*
- *Do you have a clear sense of your own personal space? Are you able to set your boundaries and claim your space?*
- *How do you influence others? Do you allow others to influence you?*
- *What is your relationship with intimacy?*
- *Are you open to collaboration and finding solutions to problems?*
- *Who do you need to confront?*
- *What aspects of yourself do you need to confront?*

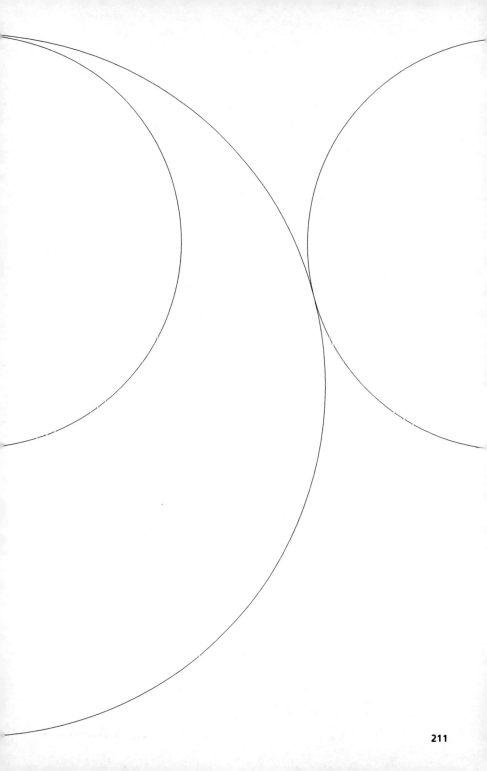

THE PRACTICE OF
RESPECTFUL
DEFENSE

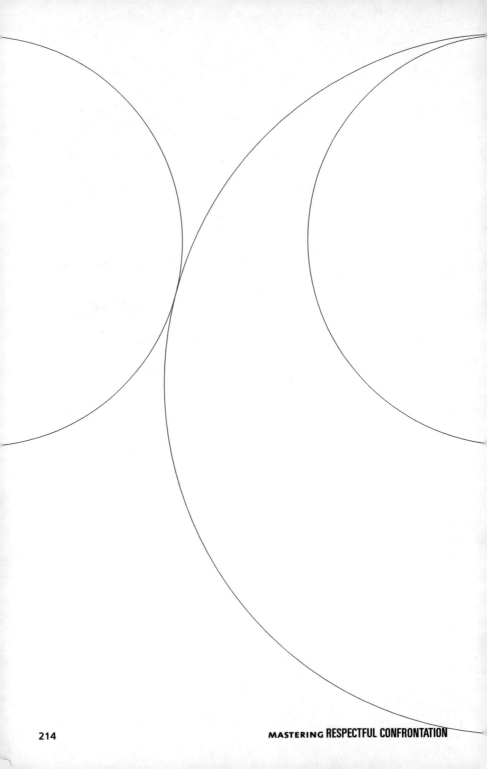

MASTERING RESPECTFUL CONFRONTATION

THE DILEMMA

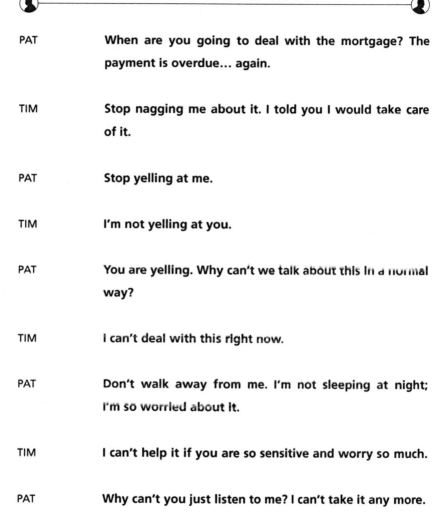

PAT When are you going to deal with the mortgage? The payment is overdue… again.

TIM Stop nagging me about it. I told you I would take care of it.

PAT Stop yelling at me.

TIM I'm not yelling at you.

PAT You are yelling. Why can't we talk about this in a normal way?

TIM I can't deal with this right now.

PAT Don't walk away from me. I'm not sleeping at night; I'm so worried about it.

TIM I can't help it if you are so sensitive and worry so much.

PAT Why can't you just listen to me? I can't take it any more.

TIM You think you are the only one having a tough time?...

"I never dealt with difficult issues because I was afraid of my own anger. I now see that I can be angry in a healthy way and not run the risk of hurting people. I feel free to express myself and be more of myself."

UNDERSTANDING THE POWER OF DEFENSE

Up until now, we have explored:

- *How to tap into your true power*
- *How to get centered and present*
- *The basic rules and foundation of communication*
- *How to assert feelings and needs from a place of openheartedness and balance*
- *How to set boundaries*

With these new skills, you will be able to confront those who are willing to be openhearted and those who share these same techniques, values, and viewpoints. Like a martial artist, you are sparring with other students from your group in a fun, open, and respectful way. You play by the same rules and know the same strategies of offense; there is very little chance that these sparring matches will lead to conflict or real combat.

In reality, most of the interactions you have are with people who don't know these techniques and who aren't committed to interacting with people in an openhearted way. They probably aren't even aware that their behavior could lead to conflict, unresolved resentment, and anger, or that their behavior may even be perceived as harmful.

Staying engaged and not getting hurt in the process with real-life confrontations requires clear and powerful techniques. The Practice of Respectful Defense requires *courage* to ensure that the interaction moves toward collaboration as opposed to conflict, as well as the *wisdom* to know when it is appropriate to stay engaged and when it is smart to end the connection. With Respectful Offense, you utilize the power of strength and the masculine principle; with Respectful Defense you bring in all the skillful tactics of the power of flexibility and the feminine principle.

At this point in the training, the martial arts student will learn defense techniques. He will feel confident to stay in the match without getting hurt or defeated because he is equipped to anticipate the attacks of the opponent and then have clear strategies to deal with these attacks. Defending yourself is not a sign of weakness, but an empowered way to engage with confidence, strength, courage, and wisdom. When you feel confident to defend yourself and still stay open to the other, you will take big risks, have a positive impact, and find personal freedom and fulfillment. *The key to this practice is the ability to stay open to the other even when you may have to defend yourself.*

The more you reveal your truth, the more likely the other may react or behave in an unconscious way. Hearing the truth is challenging and uncomfortable because it often leads to change and deeper levels of intimacy. The unconscious, reactive things we do, or don't do, keep us from getting to the truth, cause conflict and confusion, disempower others, and create distance in relationship. This is the true "enemy" in the practice of openhearted engagement, not the person!

These enemies that lead to harmful thoughts, speech, and actions are the primary causes of aggression. And when you think about it, we all do it! St. Francis of Assisi said, "No one is to be called an enemy, all are your benefactors, and no one does you harm. You have no enemy except yourselves." The more you know the workings of these enemies, the easier it will be to disarm them, avoid getting hurt, harm others, and know when it is appropriate to remove yourself from a confrontation.

IDENTIFYING THE TRUE ENEMY

Let's take a deeper look at this enemy and how it manages to infiltrate so much of our lives. Keep an open mind in this exploration. Approach this without judgment and with a certain level of humor. Like everyone else on this planet, you commit acts of aggression. You may not physically harm others with sharp objects, but this enemy of unconscious reactive behavior has many faces.

RESPECTFUL CONFRONTATION AND WORLD PEACE

I am very inspired by the life and philosophies of the Peace Pilgrim. Born Mildred Lisette Norman, the Peace Pilgrim was a peace activist who began walking across the United States in 1953 and continued for twenty-eight years, walking more than 25,000 miles, until her death in 1981. She had taken a vow to remain a wanderer until mankind had learned the way of peace. She walked until given shelter and fasted until given food. Spending much of her time writing beautiful treatises on peace and personal responsibility, she advocated the following principle: "This is the way of peace: Overcome evil with good, and falsehood with truth, and hatred with love."

One of the central beliefs in her philosophy is that we *will never end world war and strife until each one of us look at our own personal, psychological violence and take steps to eliminate it.* This statement has deep implications. What she is inferring is that even though many of us may have good intentions and live a "moral" life, we still hold on to many unconscious disturbing emotions, beliefs, and reactive patterns that adversely influence our behavior and how we engage with others.

We have the intelligence and capabilities to solve many of our personal and global problems, yet we continue to repeat old patterns that cause separation and arguments. The crime rate continues to climb; we still fight and hold on to grudges to those around us. Even those who try to be responsible citizens of the world, and who advocate for peace and social justice, still have trouble cooperating with others, maintaining healthy relationships, and fall short in creating effective, lasting change.

You see this often in non-profit and charity organizations and spiritual groups. They may have a clear philosophical goal, noble values, and a strong desire to improve individual and societal problems, but when it comes to how the companies function internally on a day-to-day basis, you see a lot of anger, resentment, personal dissatisfaction and mis-understanding. This leads to the breakdown in structure and productivity of the group, as well as high anxiety levels of the members.

These well-meaning people may hold high spiritual and noble values that shape their outward selves, but that doesn't mean they have done the more personal inner work of overcoming their own aggression,

MASTERING RESPECTFUL CONFRONTATION

anger, confusion, attachments, fears, and insecurities. These unconscious tensions build up over the years. This build up of disturbing energy is like a pot of boiling water that has a tight lid on it. Over many years of arguments, unspoken truths, unexpressed feelings and needs, trauma, and resentment, the pressure builds and builds. If you don't find ways to let off the steam, you will eventually explode, or you will start "cracking" and the "steam" will find ways to seep out.

RESPECTFUL CONFRONTATION AND YOUR BODY

Western science has proven that the nervous system stores unresolved emotions and old experiences that have not been fully expressed, as well as habits, belief systems, and trauma. Candace Pert, former Chief of Brain Biochemistry at the National Institute of Health in the United States, studied the inner workings of the body with an eye towards identifying and locating the chemistry of emotions. She said, "There is a lot of evidence that memory occurs at the point of the synapse in the neurons. One cell communicates with another. And we know that at the synapse, there are changes that take place in the receptors. The sensitivity of the receptors is part of memory and pattern storage. But the peptide network extends to organs, tissue, skin, muscle and endocrine glands. They all have peptides receptors on them and can access and store emotional information. This means the emotional memory is stored in many places in the body, not just the brain. The autonomic nervous system is pivotal to this entire understanding."

When these experiences are resolved and released from the body, the nervous system can function in a proper way, promoting good health and releasing the hormones necessary to bring about a state of calm, ease, and flow. However, many of us haven't resolved these inner conflicts. Like the boiling pot, they keep building and manifest as stress, anxiety, physical tension, chronic pain, and addiction until the body can't take it any more and they eventually seep out or explode out. When we are not mindful, we unconsciously allow these tensions to adversely influence our behavior and how we connect with others.

When the tension explodes out, it usually looks like temper tantrums and physical violence, as well as emotional tormenting and taunting. I call this *high-grade aggression*. Since the seeping out of unresolved tension is subtler, it is harder to detect and may not even be considered violence. Some examples of aggression that seeps out are gossiping, insults, passive-aggressive statements, arriving late to an appointment, and not calling when you say you will. All the small things you do or say, or don't do or say, that hurt or aggravate someone can be considered psychological violence. I call this *low-grade aggression*.

Whether conscious or unconscious, both types of unconscious aggressive behavior tend to cause pain to others, and create tension, separation, and the disempowerment of others. Both manage to keep you from being in your heart because you hold on to resentment, judgment, and fear when connecting to others. *This is the true enemy and the very thing that we must deal with in order to find personal freedom and use empowered collaboration to deepen relationship and create positive change.*

You may not think that a little bit of gossip can be just as destructive as bombing a village, but think about the number of times you gossip. Think about all that gossip building up and causing other types of aggression. Before you know it, all of these small, low-grade, violent acts result in the end of a relationship, the dissolution of a company, crime, domestic violence or gang warfare.

I did consulting for a company where gossip was a common way of engaging with one another. This caused tension between the employees and created cliques, resulting in important information not being communicated to the right people. Over time, some of the workers began to develop stress-related illnesses and many mistakes were made—like clients were not given correct times for appointments and bills were being paid twice. The gossip had become so commonplace at this company that one morning the receptionist made fun of a client to a colleague and forgot that the husband of this client was still in the office. He, of course, heard everything. The receptionist was fired and the client never came back and started saying bad things about the company.

RESPECTFUL CONFRONTATION AND PERSONAL CHOICE

How do we intend to tackle the big world challenges if we can't yet manage our own unconscious, reactive behavior? Turn the focus inward and start with yourself. Take care of your own low-grade aggression; this will take you a lifetime. There are those in the world who don't have the opportunity to resolve these issues. People in war zones, with a history of severe trauma, or who have strong, psychological disabilities are aggressive because they are lost in their unresolved traumas, bombarded with systematic abuse, or they are victims of chemical imbalances.

You have the choice to make a difference. Start with changing your viewpoints. Stop blaming others for your problems and relying on statistics, the media, politicians, and the police to solve all the strife and distress in the world. Overcome your judgments, addictions, disturbing emotions, reactive behavior, and become more mindful of your thoughts, words, and actions.

Eliminating low-grade aggression begins with first noticing what you do that causes separation, anxiety, and tension to yourself and others. Becoming familiar with your unconscious habits is the first step in the process of changing the patterns that hold you back from growth, healing, and unity. *Stay mindful, aware and present, so when the aggression starts, you can make new choices.* By doing so, you slowly develop new habits that bring about connection and the empowerment of all involved. St. Francis of Assisi said, "Above all the grace and the gifts that Christ gives to his beloved is that of overcoming self."

What aggressive things do you think, say, and do? Take the time to confess! The following exercise will help to you to recognize your own aggression, and actually put it into words, as a way to release the built-up tensions that cause the psychological violence. Many of us have negative associations with the idea of confession. I believe that confession is a healthy way to release the causes of aggression with mindfulness and love, leading to renewed energy and emotional freedom. When you confess, you take responsibility for your part in the problems in your own personal life. According to Buddhist teachings, confession is a powerful practice that leads to remorse and the resolve to not repeat the act and perpetuate the problem.

In this context, confession is not meant to make you feel guilty and shameful but to help you see that you are just as human and complex as anyone else. This idea opens you to others with empathy and compassion. It may even help you to forgive yourself and others so you may reclaim your true openhearted power and free yourself from resentment, hatred, and fear. Carolyn Myss, holistic healer and best-selling author, said, "The forgiving heart is capable of anything. I believe that deeply. When you forgive another, you take back the power that you have given them."

EXERCISE
FESS UP!

**BEFORE YOU START THIS EXERCISE, REVIEW
"HOW TO USE THIS BOOK" ON PAGE 23**

PRELIMINARY STEPS

(see APPENDIX ONE on page 281 for details)

▷ **Choose a good time and location**

▷ **Start with the basic sitting pose**

▷ **Bring your attention to your center**

▷ **Place all of your attention on your breath**

MAIN STEPS

▸ **Get some paper or a journal and a pen**

If you enjoy drawing, you may want to get pens of different colors.

▸ **List your own aggressive acts–actions, words, and thoughts**

Write down all the things you do, say or think that you would now consider violent or aggressive, conscious or unconscious. This could be something you do or don't do. Be radically honest. Don't spare yourself. No one needs to see this list; keep it secret. You may even want to throw it away when you are done. Take a few days and keep adding to the list. You will be surprised what comes up.

Here are some suggestions: *What kind of a driver are you? Do you say you'll call someone and then don't? Do you criticize others as a way to make them feel a bit insecure? Do you gossip? Do you abuse your body with food or overworking?*

▸ **Observe others and list their aggressive acts**

Be sure not to judge them; simply observe. *Ask yourself honestly if you do the same thing.* You'll be surprised.

▸ **Notice how this makes you feel**

Review your lists. Allow any feelings to flow. Write down anything that comes up. See what this new information reveals in terms of how you view yourself. Do you feel any remorse for your actions? Do you find yourself forgiving others for their actions?

▸ **Write down any decisions you make and any strategies for changing your habits.**

By committing to change your habits, you will slowly transform yourself and have a positive effect on those around you.

CLOSING STEPS

(see APPENDIX ONE on page 283 for details)

▷ **Shake out and stretch your legs**
▷ **Make notes on what you have discovered**

RECOMMENDED SCHEDULE

You may find that doing this exercise once is enough. You could make it a regular mindfulness practice. Checking in and evaluating your actions daily, weekly or monthly will more effectively result in overcoming unconscious, reactive behavior, and lead to more peace and fulfillment.

A CLOSE LOOK AT ANGER

Not all aggression looks the same. Any act, word or gesture that pierces through into someone else's personal space and causes the other to feel unsafe, threatened or hurt is considered aggression. That could be a look, shouting, pulling a gun or ignoring someone.

We have many unclear and inaccurate views about anger, causing long-term conflicts, stress, and illnesses. Many of us believe that aggression always includes violence, that all aggression comes from anger, and that all anger is aggressive. On its own, anger is not necessarily aggression. Let's take a look at anger from different angles.

All religions, therapists, doctors, and many others have something to say about anger. Looking at history, you can see how it has played a role in human events. It seems to be something that we all encounter—that we all have within us—and that we all need to either overcome or embrace. Most of us will agree that unchecked, unbridled anger is destructive and should be overcome. The Buddha said, "Holding on to anger is like grasping a hot coal with the intent of throwing it at someone else; you are the one who gets burned."

There is healthy anger and unhealthy anger. Anger is only aggressive when it explodes or seeps out unconsciously and harms, violates or disempowers others. When anger does not influence another in a harmful way, it is simply a healthy expression of your deeper feelings and passions. Expressing anger in a healthy way can lead to creativity, motivate you to take action, and help you access your personal power. Early twentieth century, American Congregationalist theologian and author Lyman Abbot said, "Do not teach your children never to be angry; teach them how to be angry well."

Because we were not encouraged to express our anger in a healthy way, we were taught to hold it in and not express it. Over the years, as this tension builds in the body, we get cut off from our creativity, power, and ability to connect in an openhearted way. The human body and psyche can only take so much tension, anxiety, and blocked energy before it somehow needs to be released.

When you choose to express anger consciously in an environment that is therapeutic or safe, you let off necessary steam as a way to avoid it exploding or leaking out at inappropriate moments. By doing so, you avoid the reactive outbursts that you oftentimes regret afterwards.

Think of a balloon. If it has too much air, it will eventually explode. If you let the air out without holding on to the opening, it can get out of your hands and fly all over the place. However, if you have a strong hold on the opening and choose to let it out in small amounts, you maintain control of how much air is released. Like the balloon, *if you are in control of releasing your anger instead of letting the emotions take control of you, no one gets hurt.*

- *What is your relationship with anger?*
- *How does it manifest in your life?*
- *Do you have a temper?*
- *Do you get irritated?*
- *Do you turn your anger inward and harm yourself?*

You may be the type who can easily express anger, someone who has never expressed anger or maybe somewhere in between. Not expressing anger doesn't mean you don't get angry.

There are many constructive ways to release your anger and old,

MASTERING RESPECTFUL CONFRONTATION

unresolved pains and experiences that may be blocking your natural flow of energy. Grab a pillow and bang your bed. Go to the beach or the woods by yourself and scream as loud as you can. Do some rigorous, physical activities, like gardening or shoveling snow. These are some examples of how to release pent-up energy.

As a preventative strategy, you are taking responsibility for your own actions and state of mind. You are learning how to be angry in a healthy way if you can teach yourself to recognize when anger is rising and then find a way to express it that doesn't feel aggressive to another. The important point here is to train yourself to not direct your anger towards someone else. *Anger in itself is not harmful. How we use our anger is.*

Another way to view anger is to see it as a *signpost* for what is happening internally with you or someone else. In The Practice of Respectful Defense, using anger to gauge the state of being of someone is a skillful way to succeed when you are confronting challenging issues. In my observations with people from around the world, people generally get angry when they feel *helpless, powerless* or that they are *not being understood.*

Take a look at past moments when you or someone else was angry. Usually you will discover that under all the confusion and heated emotions, the person who was angry somehow felt that they had no way out. They felt trapped, powerless, paralyzed or frustrated that no one was listening to what they were saying or needing.

When you view anger in this way, you will be more likely to succeed in avoiding conflict, reactive behavior, and separation. *Instead of engaging with the anger, stay centered and don't take it personally.* This higher approach to anger and aggression will transform your life and your relationships. It is the anger that is harmful, not the person. Show compassion and understanding to the one who is angry and ask yourself, "Why is that person feeling powerless, helpless or misunderstood?" When you find an answer, make an effort to listen more and let him know that you are there to support him, hear him, and help him find his way back to empowerment.

Don't be afraid of anger! See it as a rich and powerful way to express yourself. Like other emotions that we tend to avoid, like fear and sorrow, anger is part of our human condition and something we all have in common. In the process of Respectful Confrontation, it is your task to examine all of who you are, even the unpleasant parts of you. By doing so, you free yourself of the patterns that cause you to be reactive and aggressive. You integrate all of who you are leading to wholeness, balance, depth, and freedom.

"I think one of the most useful things in this practice is seeing my own violence and how that causes some of the struggles in my family. I never saw myself as someone who avoids the truth. I now feel like I have ways to identify some of the behavior of my husband and the kids. This helps me to know how to respond when they get into their stuff. We are arguing less and talking more."

UNDERSTANDING AGGRESSION

Unfortunately, twenty-first century life is harsh, with crime, war, and strife as common parts of our existence. To engage in an openhearted way without getting harmed requires courage and the ability to protect yourself from the realities of these challenging times. The better you understand aggression, the easier it will be to defend yourself. The more confident you feel that you can defend yourself from the conscious and unconscious behavior of others, the more confidence you will have to confront and speak your truth. American Ninja master Stephen Hayes said, "The idea of fearlessness does not mean bravado or recklessness. It means knowing your limitations, avoiding certain situations, and working with the situations that are inevitable." *The power of Respectful Confrontation lies in the ability to stay in the confrontation and succeed in speaking your truth even if the other uses aggression.*

The Practice of Respectful Defense helps you to identify the different types of aggression so you will know which strategies to use at any given moment of your confrontation. Aggression is any kind of action, gesture or words (or absence of these) that enter the personal space of another resulting in the other having an adverse, unpleasant reaction. This could be almost anything! In The Practice of Respectful Offense, we explored how assertiveness and aggression are almost the same. You could have good intentions and think that you are asserting, but the effect of your actions could be misinterpreted or misunderstood.

Let's look at an example: a smile. Is a smile assertive or aggressive? It all depends on the context. Imagine a young girl doing a recital at school. She is very nervous and feels like she will mess up. Just before she starts, she glances out into the audience and sees her mother smiling at her. With that smile, the young girl's mother has *asserted* her love and pride in her daughter, touching her heart and uplifting her. She plays beautifully.

Now let's look at that same smile, different context. A woman is standing at a bar with some friends having a good time. She looks to the other end of the bar to see a man staring at her with a sly, penetrating smile. She looks away and tries to connect with her friends. He continues to stare not breaking his gaze from her, smiling. She can't seem to focus on her friends anymore; he has entered her personal space, even though he is on the other side of the bar. She begins to feel uncomfortable, maybe even violated. She is no longer having a good time. This is *aggression.*

When you recognize that most of human interaction includes aggression, both low-grade and high-grade, then you can see how important it is to have clear strategies to protect yourself while still engaging with understanding and respect. It would not be smart or safe to be equally open with every person you encounter. *By holding yourself accountable for your own low-grade aggression and shining a light on the low-grade aggression of those around you, you have an opportunity to eliminate the actual causes that lead to miscommunication, conflict, injustice, and eventually crime and war.*

Like the experienced, skilled martial artist, you are ready to assert yourself fully. You stand strong, engage in an openhearted way, and recognize when your own personal space and boundaries are being threatened so you can quickly find an appropriate defense to stop it. In order to feel confident that you can defend yourself from the aggression of others, you must have a clear understanding of the different levels of aggression, the many creative ways that aggression is used to avoid the uncomfortable process of confrontation, and effective tools to address them without getting hurt or defeated.

This is an exciting part of the training, where you learn skills and defensive strategies to take whatever comes your way and turn it to your advantage. The more you understand the intricacies of offense and defense, the more you can *use* the behavior of the other to follow through with asserting your truth. Review Understanding the Masculine and Feminine Principles on page 94 to see how defense, flexibility, and the feminine principle can be used to empower your confrontations.

So let's get started and get to know our "enemy" by breaking down aggression into three levels. Remember, aggression is any action, gesture, word or silence that is used to avoid speaking or hearing the truth, and *to avoid the discomfort of being vulnerable and confronting important issues.* Also, the acts of aggression in all three levels may be conscious or unconscious and the actions of a healthy person or a psychologically challenged person.

The point is to classify the behavior, not judge or condemn it, so you can assess what level of protection you need *to stay engaged*. To best protect yourself and avoid conflict, *you must catch the signs before they take hold.* **We will look at each level of aggression, from most severe to least, and I will explain:**

- *What they generally look like*
- *How to recognize them*
- *And defensive strategies for engaging with and confronting them*

HIGH-GRADE AGGRESSION

DESCRIPTION

High-grade aggression includes physical violence and abuse where your safety or well-being is a real issue. Someone could be coming at you with a knife. It could be a very drunk person or a person who has a history of physical violence or psychological imbalances. When someone is approaching you with high-grade aggression, they are completely violating your boundaries.

HOW TO RECOGNIZE IT

It is usually not difficult to recognize the signs of this type of aggression. Even if the action is subtle, you will feel frightened, violated, and threatened.

DEFENSIVE STRATEGY: "NO!"

The best defensive strategy for dealing with this person is to *run!* You may have important things to say, but this is not the right moment. After a clear assessment of the situation, you conclude that trying to engage is not going to have any positive results and will probably result in physical harm; he is probably not even capable of hearing your truth. If you choose to stay engaged and not remove yourself from the situation, you will not only get hurt, but you are giving him an opportunity to be violent. If this were someone with whom you already have a relationship, I still advise you to remove yourself from immediate danger and deal with the issue you want to confront when and if he becomes more reasonable and approachable.

I call this defensive strategy the "No!" strategy. The exclamation mark implies that there is no room for discussion. Your "no" is final. Based on the behavior of the other, you conclude that the most appropriate choice is to protect your own personal space. You may not actually say the word "no," but your actions are saying, "at this moment, no further engagement is possible." Even though the ultimate goal of Respectful Confrontation is to stay engaged until resolution is found, sometimes retreat is the wisest choice.

Hopefully you won't have to defend yourself from high-grade aggression too often. In fact, the majority of the tools of Respectful Confrontation are designed to keep your interactions from escalating to this point.

While the best defensive strategy for high-grade aggression is to disengage from the other, there may be times when you can use skillful means to stay engaged in some creative way that will still give you the feeling that you are fulfilling your oath to have compassion and understanding for all beings and also ensure that you don't get hurt. How you do this is up to you.

Yes, the ultimate goal of Respectful Confrontation is to have open-hearted connection with all beings. But the level of opening to others must be determined by *how well you are taking care of yourself.* Your mastery of presence, centeredness, and true power determines your capacity for opening to others including friends, adversaries, and strangers. Until you have mastered these skills, use the strategy of "No!" when appropriate.

EXAMPLE

Here is an example of how I have been able to maintain an open-hearted engagement with someone I felt may have caused me harm:

One night, I was walking on a dark street in a big city. On the other side of the street was a man who was screaming at himself or at some unseen beings with whom he was angry. He wasn't wounded, but he seemed unstable. I had to get to my car, which meant I had to walk by him. I quickly assessed that it would have been a bad idea for both of us if he noticed me.

"How do I stay engaged with him?" I asked myself. I decided to cross the street and keep my distance. I didn't look at him. I walked passed him, keeping my distance, aware of my personal boundary, and without getting his attention. While I did this, I began to offer him blessings. I opened my heart and wished him good will, health, and balance. I prayed for his protection. I made it to my car safely and I continued to bless him as I drove away.

I wish I could have done more for him. However, upon evaluating the situation, my strategy seemed the most appropriate action. Someone else may have chosen another way to do it. There are many possibilities.

One sign of wisdom is to know what you have the capacity to influence or not influence *at this moment*. When you start with the things you can influence and those things that are closest to you in your immediate surroundings, you will discover that you are suddenly positioned to have the power to influence things you never thought you could.

MEDIUM-GRADE AGGRESSION

DESCRIPTION

Medium-grade aggression is a bit subtler than high-grade aggression. In high-grade aggression, the other has clearly stepped into your personal space and has violated your boundaries. In medium-grade aggression, you have most likely been engaging with the other in an openhearted way with clear communication, but the other suddenly slips into her reactive behavior in a way that makes you feel like your boundaries and personal space *run the risk* of being violated.

Some examples of medium-grade aggression are:
Getting physically too close, a raised voice, verbal intimidation, silence, raising the volume of the music so as not to be able to hear what you have to say, making accusations, walking out of the house when you are talking, saying things that insult you or throw you off, confusing you or making you feel insecure, and continuing to ask for more when you have already established what you are prepared to give.

These may be actions that you do or see every day. According to this practice, if the actions run the risk of entering your personal space in a way that is inappropriate, uninvited or cause harm, they are considered medium-grade aggression. Think about moments in the past when you tried to assert your feelings and needs and the other person, frightened of hearing the truth, used tactics to hurt you or throw you off. The more challenging the confrontation, the cleverer the unconscious or conscious tactics will be to derail you. Someone who knows you well knows all of your triggers and will use them to distract you.

HOW TO RECOGNIZE IT

Unlike high-grade aggression, there may be no real threat of violence, yet you still feel that the other has gone too far or is about to go too far. You *begin* to feel unsafe, not valued, and disrespected, *but not to the point that you feel your safety is an issue*. If you let the other continue with this behavior, it may escalate to violence, it may derail you from speaking your truth or you find yourself in old patterns of fighting or shutting down. There is no clear *external* way to know if the other is committing medium-grade aggression because *your feeling determines if the other has gone too far or not.*

In order to fully understand medium-grade aggression, I recommend you review the chapter Personal Space on page 181. The more clarity you have on boundaries and personal space, the more skillful you will be in recognizing and defending yourself from medium-grade aggression.

DEFENSIVE STRATEGY: "NO, AND…"

The goal of defending yourself from medium-grade aggression is to overcome obstacles to speaking your truth and to ensure that the behavior of the other doesn't escalate to high-grade aggression.

The defensive strategy for engaging with medium-grade aggression is to:

- *Stay engaged; there is no need to retreat or end the communication*
- *Protect your boundaries and personal space*
- *Continue asserting your truth*

I call this the "No, and…" defensive strategy. In high-grade aggression, with the "No!" defensive strategy, the exclamation point implies that the discussion is over; there is no room for negotiation. With "No, and..." you are communicating that you are still prepared to continue engaging *only if* the other stops the thing they are doing. You are not saying "no" to *them*, but to the *behavior, gesture or words* that are disturbing you.

From the perspective of martial arts, addressing high-grade aggression is like running off of the mat and ending the match. Defending yourself from medium-grade aggression is like blocking the opponent's attack. When you block an attack, you stand strong and defend yourself from the force of the other's impact. Instead of it landing on your face or in your gut, you use your arms or legs to protect yourself or you make sure the blow misses you. You stop the assault before it enters into the most vulnerable part of your personal space.

When you are confronting someone, you defend yourself from medium-grade aggression to make sure that the other's behavior doesn't violate your boundaries, hit you in your most vulnerable place, and trigger your reactive behavior. This doesn't have much to do with the physical body, but more with your emotions.

The most effective way to defend yourself from medium-grade aggression is to stop the behavior of the other before it crosses over into your personal space. You may actually say "no" to the other or you may imply that what they are doing has to stop with a simple request like "please take a step back," or "please lower your voice" or "I've had enough." No matter what you do or say, the bottom line message is "no."

Saying "no" and still choosing to connect gives a powerful signal to the other that you truly value the relationship *and* that you can take care of yourself. This defensive strategy will give a feeling of empowerment and trust and will come in handy as you continue to get to the heart of the issue that you are confronting. Remember, the other is probably not mindful; she will behave in a reactive way to avoid being uncomfortable or hearing your truth. You should expect it. Your success lies in how effective you are in addressing her behavior before it escalates.

This requires skill in presence, centeredness, true power, clear awareness of personal space, communication, and proficiency in the vocabulary of feelings and needs. You assert your truth clearly, block all attempts to distract you, and stay grounded and focused in order to reach your goal. If you have clearly stated that the behavior of the other is threatening your boundaries and personal space, and she continues to do it, then make another attempt with the "No, and…" defensive strategy. If she still continues with this behavior knowing that it is unpleasant for you, *she is now committing high-grade aggression*. At this point, switch to the appropriate defensive strategies and end the interaction.

EXAMPLE

In the past, I was terrified to say "no." I somehow believed that if I said "no" that the world might fall apart or that I would be abandoned, rejected, disrespected or that the other would crumble. It was hard to say "no" because I saw it as final.

My mother was a great person for me to learn from to set boundaries and say "no." For instance, when she would call me on the phone, ninety-five percent of our conversations were taken up with her complaining about her life. After many years of this, I'd had enough. I felt ignored and our talks always left me with a bad feeling. It was time to confront her. Confronting my mother was no easy task!

During our next phone call, she started her usual pattern of complaining. I mustered up the courage to speak my truth and assert my feelings and needs. I made it clear to her that I had sympathy for her problems. I said to her that I was no longer prepared to listen to her complain, and

I was completely available day or night to brainstorm with her to find creative ways to solve her problems. At first she was very upset, but after many talks she was able to see that I wanted to help and stay engaged as long as she stopped the complaining. I was offering her an option. It took many years before she was able to change her habit of complaining with me. However, because of my clear "No, and..." defensive strategy she found ways to improve her life and our relationship deepened.

Discovering that I could say "no" and still stay engaged was an eye-opener. How empowering to know that I could state my boundaries and still honor the other by including the "and" with my "no." This is inviting and empowering, not threatening and antagonistic. This has brought me joy, freedom, strength, and clarity in my interactions with others. The exercises I use in my trainings which address our relationship with "no" have proven time and again to be transformative and liberating for many participants. I encourage you to practice it.

LOW-GRADE AGGRESSION

DESCRIPTION

Most of reactive, unconscious behavior comes under the category of low-grade aggression. Basically, low-grade aggression is any action, gesture or words, or absence of these, that are passive or active, conscious or unconscious, that are implemented in order to avoid speaking or hearing the truth or to avoid confrontation, vulnerability, and resolving challenges.

Most of low-grade aggression is reactive; we aren't even aware we are doing it. Because speaking or hearing the truth is uncomfortable, we make unconscious choices based on unexamined beliefs, habits, and negative emotions such as fear, anger, and greed. This type of aggression has a low-grade impact and may not at first violate the boundaries or personal space of another. You will find this kind of reactive behavior in most of your daily conversations and interactions. Most of it goes unnoticed by the untrained ear, and many may even say that what falls in the category of low-grade aggression is not aggression at all.

Silence and "passive aggression" are popular forms of low-grade aggression. **Some examples are:**

- *Incessantly talking and not allowing others to speak*
- *Texting in the middle of a conversation*
- *Agreeing to something knowing that you won't do it*
- *Keeping silent when someone asks for the truth*
- *Sighing with a sad face instead of stating what you are feeling*
- *Not returning phone calls*

Low-grade aggression has the potential of escalating to conflict and maybe even high-grade and medium-grade aggression. When you use low-grade aggression to distract and avoid a confrontation, you may have won this "round" by avoiding addressing challenging issues, but the pressure mounts, the resentment builds, and the frustration creates more cracks in the relationship until you are forced to engage in a full-on "match". At that point, it may already be too late to repair the damage. Defending yourself from low-grade aggression is the most effective way to avoid your interactions leading to conflict, separation, and the breakdown of relationship. *The best strategy is prevention!*

HOW TO RECOGNIZE IT

We all have thousands of ways that we consciously and unconsciously use low-grade aggression. With so many possibilities, it is hard to recognize and offer clear strategies to defend yourself against all of them. By grouping all types of low-grade aggression into three headings, it is easier to recognize the behavior, understand the motivation behind it, and eventually come up with clear strategies to defend yourself.

To explain low-grade aggression, I have incorporated a well-known classification of reactive behavior, "Acute Stress Response" or the "3 F's". Used extensively in business theory and cultural diversity, and first introduced by American physiologist Walter Bradford Cannon in the early 1900s, the "3 F's" illustrate a general adaptation and sympathetic response to stress.

The three types of low-grade aggression are:
- **FIGHT**, *or attack*
- **FLIGHT**, *or avoidance*
- **FREEZE**, *or submission*

We will look at how we use these three types of unconscious, reactive behavior to deal with the stress of confrontation, vulnerability and change.

These impulsive responses are such a fundamental part of our lives that we don't even notice them. As children, we learned reactive patterns from our parents and culture that helped us avoid confrontation, intimacy, and uncomfortable situations. Because these patterns actually worked, we kept doing them and never questioned whether they were healthy or not. The bottom line is *we all do it!*

THE 3 F'S OF LOW-GRADE AGGRESSION

Let's start with FIGHT. The motivation of "fight", whether conscious or unconscious, is to use actions, gestures or words to intimidate, to bully or to put the other into a state of panic or confusion. "No, I won't..." is the underlying subtext. As you confront and speak your truth, the other is ready to go into combat, resist, and maintain the control of the situation.

This is usually done with raising the voice, using big gestures, pulling faces, throwing things, picking a fight, and making insults. People who use "fight" as a strategy usually get angry quickly and use intense emotions as a way to distract and throw others off balance. Feeling that they are being attacked, insulted or emotionally hurt, they are usually very good at turning anything someone does or says into an argument. These "fight-ers" don't necessarily have to be physically strong; the power lies in using emotional force to get their way.

The "fight" of low-grade aggression is different from the physical violence or the violating of boundaries that you will often see in the other levels of aggression. The hint or threat of violence is enough to distract you, intimidate you or get you riled up as a way of keeping you from getting to the heart of a sensitive issue.

The second type of low-grade aggression is FLIGHT. The motivation of "flight", whether conscious or unconscious, is to use actions, gestures or words to run away, avoid staying engaged or deal with responsibility. "I don't know..." is the underlying subtext. No matter what you say or do, "flight-ers" will find a way to delay having to make a decision, commit to something or simply not engage at all.

This usually takes on the form of walking away from you in the middle of a conversation, playing with the phone or watching TV while you are talking, changing the subject, looking off into the distance, staying busy or overworking, and postponing making decisions. People who choose "flight" as their strategy of choice are usually very charming, seductive, friendly, and playful, and manage to get away with more than others. They are very hard to pin down. Their ability to be elusive and avoid making decisions is how they maintain control of situations and keep people off balance.

In some ways, "flight" is more challenging than "fight" because it is far more subtle and difficult to detect. With "fight-ers", you tend to know what you are dealing with; you have something tangible to defend yourself from. When attempting to speak your truth to a person using the reactive behavior of "flight", it is hard to keep the two of you engaged when he so artfully finds ways to disappear. This usually results in you feeling edgy and stressed, and you can slip into your reactive behavior.

Lastly, we have the low-grade aggression of FREEZE. The motivation of using "freeze", either consciously or unconsciously, is to use actions, gestures or words of submission as a way of avoiding responsibility and being held accountable. "I can't..." is the underlining subtext. No matter what you say or do, he will find a way to get out of speaking about what he needs, sharing how he feels or taking initiative. He may even agree to something, knowing full well that he will not do it. Or if he does it, he will be resentful and find some passive, subversive way to "get you back".

What the aggression of "freeze" usually looks like is someone retreating into himself when confronted. There is a sense of paralysis, panic, and a "deer in the headlights" look. The greatest tactic is silence. He may or may not look you in the eye, but either way he seems to have gone off into some "safe place" within himself. He tends to be very quiet, say very little, and is often not noticed in large crowds.

You never know where you stand with a "freez-er". He often expects you to take care of his feelings and needs, causing you frustration. He also sees himself as a victim in many situations, putting you in the role of the perpetrator.

People who use the reactive behavior of "freeze" are the true "passive-aggressives". They avoid being in their power and yet they still find hidden, behind-the-back ways to get what they want. Plus, because they retreat inside of themselves and don't give clear signals of where they stand with issues, this may cause you to feel insecure and edgy. If you are not mindful, this could lead to you becoming aggressive in response to their behavior.

"Flight" and "freeze" seem similar, but they are different. The behavior of "flight" really looks like someone trying to escape and to avoid. The behavior of "freeze" looks more like paralysis. Both are more passive than "fight".

This is a general look at low-grade aggression and unconscious, reactive behavior. We all use all three depending on the situation, other people or the intensity of what needs to be confronted. Do you recognize them in others? How have you dealt with their clever tactics in the past? What kind of people do you tend to attract to you? "Fight-ers", "flight-ers" or "freez-ers?"

And how about yourself? After some contemplation of "fight", "flight", and "freeze", choose which of the three you think you use more than the others. This is a fun process that is liberating, empowering, and healing. Knowing how you use low-grade aggression will give you a deeper appreciation for the others in your life who have to put up with your clever tactics! Enjoy discovering how creative you and others have been; *bring your low-grade aggression out into the light.* By mastering the art of confrontation and defending yourself against reactive behavior, you foster healthy relationships, deeper connection, and the growth of all involved.

ENGAGING WITH THE "THREE F'S" OF LOW-GRADE AGGRESSION

Most people who react with *"fight"* are usually very defensive. Do not use words that make them feel like you are judging them or criticizing them. Their goal is to confuse, bully, and intimidate you. Keep calm and strong; don't raise your voice and use slow gestures. Use the power of grounding to not get distracted, and the power of focus to persist with the task at hand. Use the power of strength to assert your truth in a way that is soft and cannot be taken as an attack, and use the power of flexibility to get out of the way of the line of fire. Do not take personally what they say or do.

Don't allow the other to rile you into your reactive behavior. Once the two of you are both using "fight" as your way of engaging, then you are no longer confronting, there is no longer an openhearted connection, and you will not get to the issue that needs to be addressed. He has won that round. Jewish theologian and philosopher, Abraham J. Heschel, said, "In a controversy, the instant we feel anger, we have already ceased striving for truth and have begun striving for ourselves."

Avoid getting frustrated with people who react with *"flight"*. Because of their more illusory tactics of aggression, they tend to provoke frustration and anger in others as a way to distract. If they succeed in getting you aggravated and aggressive, they now have an excuse to end the conversation. Once again, they have won this round, but not the match.

In order to not get thrown, use the power of grounding. While he is flitting around, stay centered. The most effective way to get him to address the issue you are confronting is to remember your goal and use the power of focus. Don't get clingy with a "flight" person. That will make him flee even more. Find the right balance of strength and flexibility to keep him engaged. If you assert too much or too little, you will lose him and lose all hope of confronting the issue. Talk loud and be firm to bridge the distance that he is creating. Most importantly, use the power of flexibility to keep up with anything he may do to flee. Eye contact is essential. Turn off the TV and eliminate any distractions. Your gestures should be very purposeful.

Don't let the other activate your reactive behavior of "flight" and distract you. One clever tactic he may use is to change the subject. Before you know it, you are having a twenty-minute discussion on a future vacation, enjoying the thrill of making plans, and dreaming about the warmth of the sun and sand, instead of addressing the issue you were planning on confronting. He will try to postpone the confrontation and will focus on the future or the past. Keep him in the present, at that moment, and in that place.

With *"freeze"* aggression, it is essential to be centered and use the power of grounding and focus to stay calm and peaceful. You must be careful how you initiate the power of strength. Use strength to cut through his paralysis and lack of connection, but not in a way that will cause him to further retreat into himself. Get him to trust you and find creative ways to get him to open with the power of flexibility. While you need to be firm and assertive to reach him, come from a place of vulnerability. The more you can speak from your heart and speak your feelings and your needs, the more likely he will stay engaged and follow through with the confrontation. But if he is feeling disempowered, he will do anything to avoid something as uncomfortable and truthful as a confrontation.

Empower him, but hold him accountable for his actions. By doing so, you show that you respect him and are not treating him as a victim. Help him see that he too has an impact on others and that he is powerful. However, do not get caught up too long in dealing with his fear and inadequacies. A clever way for him to avoid confronting the necessary issues is to get you to solve his problems. Before you know it, you are having a long pep talk to help him feel better and not getting to the issue. Use the power of focus to keep on track.

Don't get worked up and angry. This may reinforce his false belief that he is a victim and that everyone else is a perpetrator. Speak firmly but in a compassionate way. Keep your gestures small, and if you make physical contact be sure your contact is affirming and gentle. Ask for eye contact and have a pleasant look on your face.

DEFENSIVE STRATEGY: "YES, AND..."

Respectful Confrontation is the process of bringing the unspoken and the unseen out into the open. By not speaking the truth and by letting these unconscious aggressions persist, you are participating in the slow and steady breakdown of your relationships. *These subtle patterns of reactive behavior that cause separation and closing of the heart will continue until someone chooses to name them and bring them to light.*

With low-grade aggression, you must be able to detect when you feel the heart connection is closing, when you begin to feel devalued or disrespected or when you feel the other is retreating. If you don't address low-grade aggression *when it first starts*, it will probably throw you off, keep you from following through with your confrontation, and eventually escalate to high-grade or medium-grade aggression.

The way to defend yourself from high-grade and medium-grade aggression is to remove yourself from the situation or block the behavior to protect your personal space. Because low-grade aggression has a milder effect on the interaction, the best way to defend yourself is to actually use the action of the other! This is where we see the skill, mastery, and the true sport of Respectful Confrontation. *Instead of feeling disempowered or defeated by the aggressive behavior you actually use it to your advantage.*

I call this the "Yes, and…" defensive strategy. You say yes to what he does and use that very thing that is causing the problem to get back to connection! This is the dance of giving and receiving where a mastery of both the true powers of strength and flexibility, and the masculine and feminine principles, are essential. You use these principles to stay engaged and achieve your goal of speaking your truth.

Because low-grade aggression hasn't reached the point where your personal space feels threatened, you can stay engaged without getting hurt. Actually, the act of acknowledging and making use of the low-grade aggressive behavior in your interaction is what *keeps* you from getting hurt. When defending yourself from low-grade aggression, remember that you are addressing the *behavior or action* of the person and not the person.

The "Yes, and…" strategy relies largely on the power of flexibility to ensure that the reactive behavior of the other won't throw you like it did in the past. In fact, with flexibility you will find ways to throw it back at him, taking him off guard and shaking him into more awareness of what he is doing.

Imagine two martial artists opposing one another. When one throws a punch, the other has many choices. She can stand there and take the blow, feel the pain, and get thrown off balance. That is not a recommended strategy!

Another choice is to see the blow coming and at the last minute step out of the way (flexibility) causing her opponent to fall forward and be off-balance. This is an ideal moment to come back with an offensive maneuver, like punching or throwing him to the floor.

A third choice is to see the punch coming, and as it gets closer, grab the hand of the opponent, pull back to soften the impact (backward-moving, receptive), actually use *his force* in the punch to push back on him, and throw him off balance. Tai Chi and higher levels of martial arts offer ways to use this power to defeat opponents.

By receiving and giving back the low-grade aggression, you don't have to use much force; you save your energy and wear out your opponent. He is not only putting out energy to try and distract you, but he now also needs energy to acknowledge and deal with his very own force!

The aggression of the other only has power if you don't acknowledge it or get distracted by it. The other may not like that his clever tactics are no longer working to avoid the confrontation, but by saying "yes" to what he does or says shows that you are acknowledging him and not ignoring him. *When you name the behavior, you are giving him back the responsibility of his own actions instead of taking it on.*

Since you will most likely be defending yourself from low-grade aggression in most of your confrontations, we will take a closer look at this useful tool of Naming the Behavior as a way to maintain openhearted connection, speak your truth, and protect yourself.

"In the past I always avoided heated discussions. I would fumble over my words. I'm finding now that I can be clear and confident in expressing my truth."

RESPECTFUL DEFENSE: NAMING THE BEHAVIOR

The following tool, Naming the Behavior, will support you in the process of protecting yourself and ensuring that the low-grade aggression of the other doesn't escalate to conflict or cause you to give up on your need to speak your truth. Taoist master Lao Tzu, said, "Respond intelligently even to unintelligent treatment."

Naming the Behavior is simple yet powerful. In fact, because it is so simple, it is sometimes hard to comprehend. Because it is so powerful and potent it requires a lot of practice to master, as well as a proficiency in the other tools of Respectful Confrontation. Imagine you are confronting someone. You are centered, present, in your true power, you have openhearted engagement, and you assert your feelings and needs. When the other gets uncomfortable, he reacts with low-grade aggression and some form of "fight", "flight" or "freeze", like raising his voice, looking at his phone or giving you a blank stare.

At this point you use the "Yes, and..." defensive strategy. Instead of ignoring the behavior, running away, or going into your own reactive behavior *you very clearly and calmly name what you see.* You are actually using the aggressive behavior of the other to disarm him and take the conversation further. You don't judge and criticize the behavior; you simply name what you see.

This may sound alien to you, really simplistic, or you may think that this cannot possibly help in defending yourself and achieving your goal. However, after many years of using and teaching this tool, I see how it has worked to empower others. The tool itself is straightforward and effective, but the execution of it is intense and requires practice. If not done correctly, your attempt could cause more damage than success. Let's break down the process.

EIGHT STEPS OF NAMING THE BEHAVIOR
....

① **START WITH CENTEREDNESS AND PRESENCE**
Review the chapter on Presence and Centeredness on page 55. Tap into your power of grounding.

② **MAKE CONTACT WITH THE OTHER AND BECOME AWARE OF THE PERSONAL SPACE OF YOURSELF AND THE OTHER**
Review the chapter on Making Contact on page 119 and the chapter on Personal Space on page 181. Tap into your power of focus.

③ **SPEAK YOUR TRUTH AND ASSERT YOUR NEEDS**
You are now in the dance of confrontation. Review the Nine Steps of Respectful Offense on page 191. Tap into your power of strength.

④ **WAIT FOR AND NOTICE THE REACTION OF THE OTHER**

After stating your truth wait to see what the reaction will be from the other. If he is open to what is being said and willing to cooperate with you, then *use the power of strength and the masculine principle to* take another step forward. If you notice that your offensive move causes him to close his heart and use strategies to avoid what needs to be confronted, *tap into your power of flexibility and the feminine principle*, stay open, and prepare to defend yourself.

(5) IDENTIFY THE REACTIVE BEHAVIOR

Classify the behavior as one of the "3 F's". Identify the exact behavior that you see. Stay grounded. This needs to be done quickly before you get derailed or distracted.

(6) PUT INTO WORDS WHAT YOU SEE

Name the behavior clearly and confidently, but not in a way that the other will feel attacked. State in one clear sentence what you notice. For instance, you could say, "I am noticing that you are raising your voice." The longer you wait, the harder it will be to be effective.

Name the exact physical thing that you see. This seems very simple, but the tool won't work otherwise. If you see him walking away, name that. If you notice him looking away, name that. If his face is getting red or his fists are clenched, name that.

(7) BE SILENT

By naming the behavior without judgment or criticism, and not getting caught up in the drama, you give him a chance to see that what he is doing is having an impact on you and that you hold him accountable for his own actions. Say, "I am noticing that you are raising your voice" and then *keep quiet*. You have one shot to make this work; one clear statement said with power and then silence.

This is critical. He is probably not even aware that he is doing this behavior. Give him the time to check in with himself and decide what he will do with this information. This requires your patience, courage, and compassion. Stand firm; don't falter. Be still and wait for his next move. *If you have communicated this effectively, he will probably recognize what he is doing, adjust, and reengage with you so you can continue with the confrontation.*

(8) **REPEAT IF NECESSARY**

If you were successful with deflecting his reactive behavior, continue with asserting your truth until the next time he feels the stress of hearing the truth and uses another type of low-grade aggression. *This dance of asserting and defending, of giving and receiving, continues until the issue you want to confront is resolved.*

....

(💡) **TIPS**

Naming someone's reactive behavior is challenging during a confrontation and when the emotions are triggered. Here are some important tips to ensure that you succeed and master this tool.

- **Don't interpret or judge.** Avoid statements like: *Why are you so angry? Don't walk away from me. You must be bored.* This may threaten him or give him ammunition to launch into a fight. If this happens, then the chances of getting to the heart of the issue are slim.

- **Speak the only truth you can speak—yours.** Starting with statements like "I am noticing..." or "It looks to me like..." or "It seems that..." helps you to stay in your power because you are speaking your truth. Saying "you are raising your voice" may or may not be true. What seems like a raised voice to one may be different for another. To him, his voice may not be loud at all. Talk to any New Yorker about loud voices! You run the risk that the other could come back with "No, I am not" and then you will probably say, "Yes, you are" and before you know it, you are in a conflict. Any attempts to get to the issues that need to be discussed in an openhearted way are gone. His strategy has worked.

However, it *is* true that it "seems to you" that he is raising his voice and that it may be making you feel uneasy. The ultimate power you have in Respectful Confrontation is your own truth!

- **Stand behind your assertion.** If the other denies that he is doing the behavior, continue with your own truth. Speaking only to what you see, and expressing your feelings and needs, keeps you in your power. Respond with something like, "Well, you may not think you are raising your voice, but it seems to me that you are, and that is making me a bit nervous." Eventually he will acknowledge the effect he is having on you and he will adapt.

If he admits that he is doing the behavior but his response is "So what? Deal with it" or "Oh, you are so sensitive," then his reactive behavior has now moved into medium-grade aggression. He has now stepped over your personal boundary. The defensive strategy for medium-grade aggression is "No, and..." which means that you can now say, "Well, when you do that behavior I don't feel safe. I'm still willing to talk to you, but my need is that you lower your voice." Again, if he is someone that is rational and with whom you have a good relationship, he will adapt.

If you find that *naming the behavior* doesn't work to change what he is doing and that *protecting your personal boundaries* doesn't work, then he is leaving you with the only safe choice: shift your defensive strategy to high-grade aggression and *end the conversation*. Take care of yourself. You may not get to the actual issue you wanted to confront, but making him aware of the impact of his aggressive behavior may have been the actual confrontation that was needed.

Respectful Confrontation is concerned with true compassion and not about being nice. Maybe you didn't get what you wanted, but you did use wisdom to protect yourself, and after some time, you may be able to address the issue again. Most likely, if you skillfully name the behavior with openness and power, he will realize that what he is doing is having an adverse impact on you and he will adjust and seek out connection.

The following exercise provides you with a structured way to practice Naming the Behavior. Before you actually use this defensive tool to confront people you know, practice alone or with someone who is also reading this book, in a safe environment.

EXERCISE

PRACTICING NAMING THE BEHAVIOR

**BEFORE YOU START THIS EXERCISE, REVIEW
"HOW TO USE THIS BOOK" ON PAGE 23**

PRELIMINARY STEPS

(see APPENDIX ONE on page 281 for details)

▷ **Choose a good time and location**

▷ **Start with the basic sitting pose**

▷ **Bring your attention to your center**

▷ **Place all of your attention on your breath**

MAIN STEPS

▶ **Get some paper or a journal and a pen**

If you enjoy drawing, you may want to get pens of different colors.

▶ **Think of all the people (or aspects of yourself) you would like to confront**

Confronting others: who do you feel that you have issues with that you would like to resolve? Who do you feel that you have closed your heart to? Who is causing you to feel disempowered or feel you can't fully be yourself? Who do you need to appreciate?

Confronting yourself: Think about certain personal character traits that you feel are holding you back or keeping you from living your true potential and capacity to be happy. This could be a habit, a belief system, a fear or an addiction.

This may trigger feelings and emotions. Allow them to flow. Don't judge yourself or the other for the behaviors that need to be confronted. Approach this exercise with an open heart.

▸ **Make a list of the reactive behavior of these people, as well as yourself**

What ways do you and the others avoid speaking and hearing truth? Be specific and stay focused on immediate behavior you can see and name like: *walking away, raising of the voice or not looking in the eyes.*

In this beginning phase, give yourself the space to write without censuring. Let your thoughts flow. Write from your heart. Nobody needs to see this. You can sort your notes later.

▸ **Group all of the behaviors on your lists under the headings:**

FIGHT | FLIGHT | FREEZE

▸ **Make lists of phrases that will work for you to name behavior**

First, choose one behavior from each of the "3 F's".

Second, make a list of two or three sentence starters that feel right to you like "It seems to me that…" or "It looks like…" or "I am noticing that…"

Third, write your complete phrases for all three behaviors.

For instance:

• *"It looks to me like you are moving away from me."*

- *"I'm noticing that you are not looking at me."*
- *"It seems to me that you are standing really close."*

Come up with phrases that seem natural to you. Use as few words as possible. Remember, you have one chance to say it and it needs to be clear, succinct, and firm. It will lose its impact if there are too many words. Make sure what you say doesn't come across as an accusation, a judgment or a criticism. That will trigger more reactive emotions.

▸ **Say the statements out loud**

Do this when you are alone or ask someone to practice with you and give you constructive feedback on how effective you are. Did your statement have a strong and openhearted impact? Were you vague, unclear or too soft?

The more you feel comfortable saying these statements when you are calm and in a practice setting, the easier it will be to say them in the heat of the moment when the emotions are high.

CLOSING STEPS

(see APPENDIX ONE on page 283 for details)

▷ **Shake out and stretch your legs**
▷ **Make notes on what you have discovered**

RECOMMENDED SCHEDULE

This tool is a potent truth teller. It is very immediate and there is no time to ease into it. Usually the emotions, fears, and past struggles are very present when you actually confront someone. To master this tool, you must practice it! A martial artist cannot take the force of her opponent and turn it back on him without years of practice. It usually takes decades to master this!

Choose three phrases and make a commitment to say each one between one hundred and one thousand times a day. This is similar to learning lines when you are rehearsing for a theatre piece. You can whisper to yourself, speak in the car when you are alone, or even when you are brushing your teeth. The more often you say these phrases, the easier it will be to say them when you are actually in the middle of a heated confrontation.

 TIPS

You can practice on your own and with others. Here are some suggestions on how to practice and develop skills in Naming the Behavior.

1 *In order to master this tool with power, clarity, and precision, review and practice the "'Hey' Exercise" on page 82 and the Five Steps to Clear Communication on page 143 .*

2 *In order to stand firm in the face of the aggression of another, review the chapter The Four Pillars of True Power on page 67. Naming the Behavior requires skill in all four powers.*

3 *In order to quickly identify one type of aggression from the other, review the chapter Understanding Aggression on page 233.*

REVIEW OF PRACTICE

You now have explored all of the components of Respectful Confrontation. You have looked through the prism to examine the many aspects of that light beam which can pierce the confusion and darkness of communication to support you on your path toward personal freedom and empowered, collaborative engagement.

You started with:
- *How to tap into your true power*
- *How to get centered and present*
- *The basic rules and foundation of communication*
- *How to assert feelings and needs from a place of openheartedness and balance*
- *How to set boundaries*

And then you played with the skills and intricacies of:
- *How to speak your truth and give feedback*
- *How to effectively acknowledge, identify, and respond to the reactive behavior of another*
- *How to collaborate and find creative solutions*

During your confrontations, you will be called to stand in your power, engage in an openhearted way, and continually shift from Respectful Offense and Respectful Defense. The power lies in your ability to listen to the subtle signals of yourself and the other. This will inform you when to move forward with speaking your truth and when you must stop to properly defend yourself from the aggression of the other. This continues until you reach your goal and finish the confrontation. The more you have mastered Respectful Confrontation, and the power of flexibility and the dance of giving and receiving, the easier it will be to solve problems, overcome personal challenges, feel empowered to live the life you choose, and support others in doing the same.

EXAMPLE OF
RESPECTFUL CONFRONTATION

JACK   Nina, do you have some time to talk?

NINA   Yeah, sure, I'm just doing some work here.

JACK   I'd rather do this when you are not distracted.

NINA   It's no big deal, go ahead.

JACK   No, this is very important to me. When will you be able to talk when I can have your full attention?

NINA   Wow, this must be serious. Well, give me a few minutes. I just have a couple of things to do and I'll be finished for the evening.

JACK   Great. Thanks.

(15 MINUTES LATER)

NINA   All done. What do you want to talk about?

JACK   I appreciate you making the time. Especially knowing how busy you are these days.

NINA   Yeah, it's a bit overwhelming.

JACK   Good, then let's keep this short. After we talk about my thing, I'd love to hear about how you are doing and what's been going on.

NINA   That sounds great.

JACK   So, as I said, what I want to talk about is really important to me. It's about the dishes.

NINA   Oh no, you must be kidding me. I finished up my work quickly so we could talk about the dishes? How can that be important?

JACK   Well, you said you were going to do them and you haven't done them.

NINA   I don't believe it! If it is so important to you, then I'll go and do them!

JACK   I'm noticing that you are raising your voice.

NINA   (Pause) Oh, I didn't realize I was raising my voice. I just get so frustrated when you keep bringing up the dishes.

JACK   I can imagine that it frustrates you. It frustrates me when you say you are going to do them and you don't.

NINA   I did do them.

JACK   In the last three weeks, you have only done them twice.

NINA   By the way, we are out of soap and juice. Someone needs to go to the store.

JACK   I'm noticing that you are changing the subject.

NINA   Well, we need those things.

JACK   Okay, I'll put that on my list and I will make sure there is soap and juice in the house by tomorrow. Do you agree with me that you only did the dishes twice in the last three weeks?

NINA   Yeah, I guess you're right. But I've told you a hundred times I am so stressed at work. Don't you hear me? You don't really know what I'm going through.

JACK   I'm noticing that you are raising your voice again.

NINA   Yeah, I'm upset.

JACK   And I want to support you. I'd be glad to listen to you, give you a chance to unwind. But let's do that after we talk about the dishes.

NINA   I can't believe you are so obsessed with the dishes. You are making such a big deal about it.

JACK   Well, this is why it is so important to me. It isn't even so much about the dishes. We made an agreement that you would do the dishes and I would do things like walk Max. I honor our commitments. When you say you are going to do something and you don't follow through, I feel like you don't respect me. I also begin to get nervous that if you don't follow through on this commitment, you may not follow through on other commitments. So, I am beginning to get insecure about our relationship.

NINA   I can't believe how sensitive you are. This isn't that big a deal.

JACK   Well, you may say that I am sensitive, but to me it is a big deal.

NINA   Wow, I didn't realize that I was having that effect on you, making you feel disrespected and insecure. I don't disrespect you and I don't want you to feel insecure. I love you.

JACK   Thank you. I love you and need to feel secure in our commitments; it's really important to me that we follow through with what we say we are going to do.

NINA   Well, I said I would do the dishes, but I am telling you now, I won't be able to do them. Not with my work schedule for the next month or so. I'm telling you now that I need my evenings free to get some extra work done. That's what I need.

JACK   (Pause) Okay, so if you don't have time in the evening to do chores, what can we come up with?

NINA   I don't know. I find that I have a bit more time in the morning.

JACK   Why don't you walk Max? I would rather sleep a little later in the morning.

NINA   I guess I could do that. Actually that would be nice. It would give me some quiet time outdoors to plan my day.

JACK   So, you walk Max in the mornings. I'll do the dishes at night.

NINA   Great.

JACK   Let's say we start tomorrow.

NINA   Okay.

JACK   Great. And can we agree that if for some reason we can't follow through with our commitment, that we will let the other know in advance and not just let it slide? Does this sound good to you?

NINA   Fine. Will that make you feel secure?

JACK   I guess so. I'll have to see how it goes in the next couple of weeks. And will this new arrangement make you feel less stressed?

NINA   Yes, definitely. I feel like a pressure has been taken off of me.

JACK   Me too. I would like to check in two weeks from now to see how this new arrangement is going. Is that fine with you?

NINA   Yeah. Good. I'm glad you were able to be so clear with what you were feeling. I didn't realize how much I was affecting you.

JACK   And I'm glad you could hear what I had to say. And I'm sorry you have had such a rough time at work. Why don't we both go and do the dishes together now and you can tell me about what is going on?

NINA   That sounds good.

BRIAN'S STORY

I have been struggling with the couple that live next door and their barking dog. I tried to tolerate it, but I couldn't any longer. It was time for me to draw my line in the sand. I did. While my instinct reaction is to feel that I am over-reacting, I have to remind myself that I get to have my feelings and I get to set my boundaries.

I found myself frozen and stuck for the whole day. As I considered options, I found my head spinning out of control picturing various scenarios. I was aware of shame and anger for not feeling confident enough to simply state my truth. So, I started preparing. I outlined my points that I would use to confront them and reviewed out loud the script of how it could go.

When the neighbor answered the door she was on the phone. I introduced myself and asked her if she had time to talk about their dog. She stated, "Well I'm on the phone." "I see that," I responded, and stated that, "If this wasn't a convenient time, could we find a convenient time, as I really needed to talk about this." She hung up the phone.

I requested that they please not leave their dog outside when they are not home. She, on a few occasions, raised her voice and got defensive. I, drawing on the memories of the practice, stayed grounded, focused, and calm. She responded back calmly.

Having prepared myself in advance, I delivered my message and then I watched to see if it was received. I simply stated the behavior and didn't make any accusations. I spoke my truth calmly. I am not a wimp.

For a few days, things were calm, but the dog was at it again. I felt very upset and physically agitated. I followed the teachings and reminded myself to not react at that time. An hour or so later, I felt grounded, so I called the neighbor at his work number and left a very short message. He returned my call and we arranged a meeting. We met at their dining room table for an hour! We had a very civil and solution-oriented discussion. Turns out we have a lot in common!

This certainly worked better than any attempts in the past. The martial arts moves and the new tools that we practiced were so helpful to me. I feel in my power! And for that, I am grateful! I can't control the outcome, but I do get to state my truth.

KEY POINTS

AGGRESSION .... ✓

THE TRUE ENEMY, UNCONSCIOUS REACTIVE BEHAVIOR .... ✓

CONFESSING PERSONAL AGGRESSION AND VIOLENCE .... ✓

ANGER .... ✓

THE THREE LEVELS OF AGGRESSION .... ✓

FIGHT, FLIGHT, AND FREEZE .... ✓

NAMING THE BEHAVIOR .... ✓

TOPICS FOR CONTEMPLATION OR JOURNALING

_____ (?)

- *How well do you feel you can defend yourself from those around you?*
- *Do you see the power in defense and the feminine principle?*
- *Do you hold onto unexpressed feeling, needs, desires, and traumas?*
- *Do you have constructive ways to release this built-up tension?*
- *What do you think, say or do that could be considered aggressive or violent? To others? To yourself?*
- *What is your relationship with anger?*
- *Are you comfortable saying "no"?*
- *Do you recognize your reactive aggressive patterns of "fight", "flight", and "freeze"? Do you recognize them in others?*
- *Do you feel confident standing face-to-face with reactive behavior?*

FINAL THOUGHTS

We are all finding our way in these times of accelerated change. To master Respectful Confrontation requires a warrior spirit, one of courage, perseverance, patience, and respect. Those with this warrior spirit choose to engage in an openhearted way and trust the power of vulnerability, love, compassion, and understanding. Buddhist teacher and peace activist, Thich Nhat Hanh, said, "Understanding shatters old knowledge to make room for the new that accords with reality."

Respectful Confrontation offers a language and system for opening up to deeper levels of understanding that will bring about personal freedom, fulfillment, and collaborative engagement.

Practice the exercises and master the skills of Developing the Respectful Self, Respectful Engagement, Respectful Offense, and Respectful Defense to find creative solutions to your personal problems and eventually create positive change in your community. By doing so, you contribute to the foundation needed to foster an era of lasting peace.

By mastering Respectful Confrontation, you open up new frontiers of personal power and self-confidence. You help usher in an era where brute force, conflict, and aggression are replaced with true power, confrontation, and assertiveness. A world where arguments, miscommunication, destructive competition, lack, war, crime, injustice, and the struggle for power make room for respect, understanding, collaboration, sharing of resources, a harmony with self, others and nature, benevolent competition, and a desire to empower others.

If you commit to making these exercises and practices a regular part of your life, you will see clear shifts in yourself and those around you! You have the choice to make a difference. Start with changing your viewpoints and relying on others to solve your problems. Overcome your judgments, disturbing emotions, and reactive behavior, and become more mindful of your thoughts, words, and actions. Stay centered, present, and in your true power. Learn to listen more deeply. Commit to speaking your truth and engaging with respect and understanding. Confront from a place of openhearted vulnerability and resolve all conflicts as quickly and skillfully as possible. This small contribution will change your relationships and help create a better world.

The hero of the twenty-first century will put down the guns, the viewpoints that create separation, the need to covet and conquer, and will place complete faith and trust in the true potential of the human spirit. This hero knows that each and every one of us is capable of the highest levels of generosity and compassion for all beings and for this planet—regardless of color, race, religion, and political affiliation. The hero of the twenty-first century engages with as many people as possible to encourage them to reveal their true power, to collaborate, and to share and receive the dreams of our enlightened future. I rejoice in the part each one of us is playing in this unfolding!

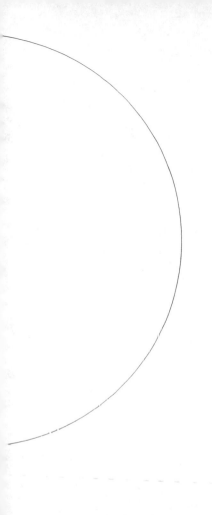

APPENDIX 1

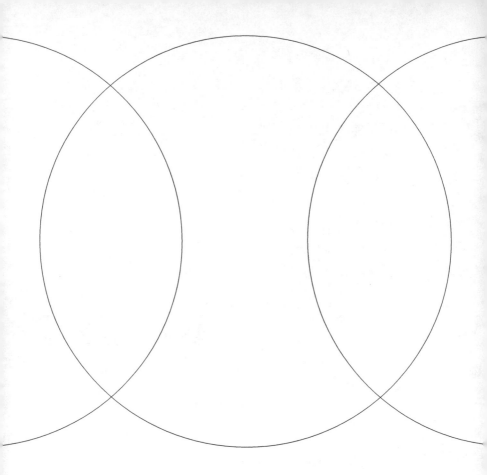

PRELIMINARY STEPS

▸ **Choose a good time and location**

Do this exercise when you are alone, or around people who can respect your need for focus and silence. Find a place to do this where there is enough space around you.

▸ **If you choose to start with the basic sitting pose**

Sit in a comfortable way. Your spine is vertical and relaxed (either sitting on a pillow on the floor with legs crossed, or sitting at the edge of a chair, feet flat on the floor); your breath is relaxed, steady and deep; your eyes are closed or partially closed looking down towards the ground; your shoulders and jaw are relaxed; your hands are resting on your knees or in your lap. This basic way of sitting allows energy to flow freely and in the long run can promote good health, looser joints, and more vitality. Hold this pose for a few minutes.

▶ **If you choose to start with the basic standing pose**

Stand with your feet apart, about the width of your hips. Keep your whole body relaxed and flexible. Bend your knees slightly. Tilt your tailbone slightly towards the front of your body. Lengthen your spine in a soft way. Lift your head lightly, and tuck your chin towards your chest. Your mouth and eyes are slightly open. This basic way of standing allows energy to flow freely and in the long run can promote good health, looser joints, and more vitality. Hold this pose for a few minutes.

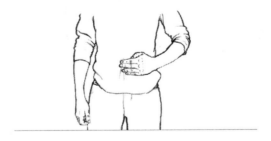

▶ **Bring your attention to your center**

Focus on a spot three finger-widths below your navel, somewhere in the center of your lower belly. Try to see this point with your mind's eye and

MASTERING RESPECTFUL CONFRONTATION

focus on it for a period of time. If you get distracted during the exercise, bring your attention back to your center to get focused.

▶ **Place all of your attention on your breath**

From your center, become aware of your breath. Breathe into your center and belly. This simple task helps you to come more into alignment with yourself and come more into the present. Breathe naturally with as little effort as possible. There is no need to change your breath. Simply notice.

CLOSING STEPS

▶ **Shake out and stretch your legs**

Stretch and shake out any tension you have acquired. You may not be doing a lot of movement, but the exercise requires a lot of exertion and energy.

▶ **Makes notes**

In order to see your progress and learn from this practice, make some notes. Don't judge yourself, only evaluate. Write down how it went and what happened. Did you learn anything new? Did you come across a new challenge? Are you seeing yourself in a new way? Make a note about how you will approach the exercise next time around.

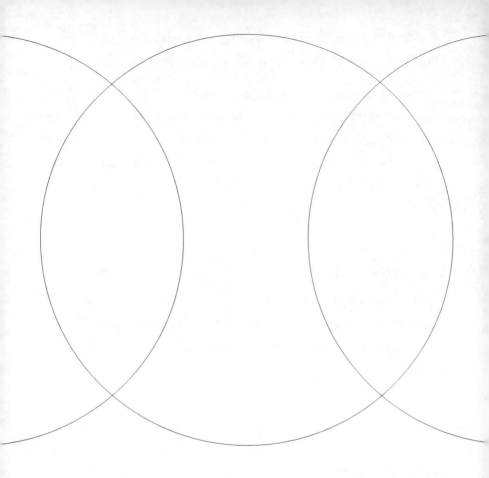

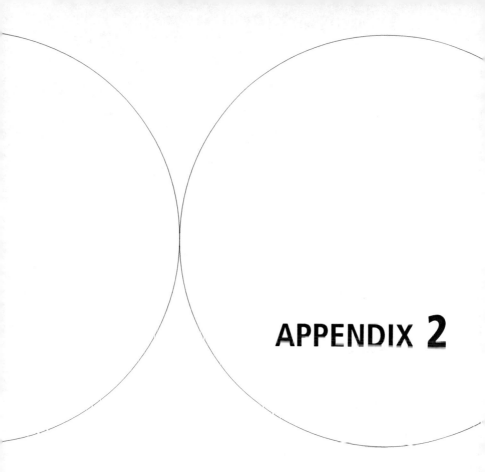

APPENDIX 2

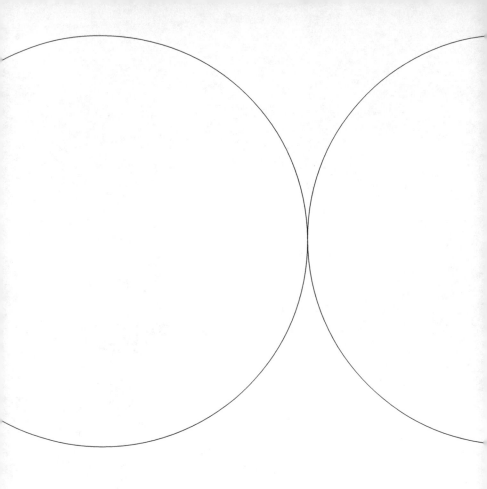

MASTERING RESPECTFUL CONFRONTATION

THE CORE EXERCISE

OPENHEARTED INTERACTION

(SEE FULL EXPLANATION OF THIS EXERCISE ON PAGE 34)

PRELIMINARY STEPS

- ▸ **Choose a good time and location**
- ▸ **Start with the basic sitting pose**
- ▸ **Bring your attention to your center**
- ▸ **Place all of your attention on your breath**

MAIN STEPS

- ▸ **Become aware of your physical body**
- ▸ **Become aware of your emotional body**
- ▸ **Become aware of your mental body**
- ▸ **Become aware of your surroundings**
- ▸ **Become aware of others**
- ▸ **Feel this in your heart with some deep breaths**
- ▸ **Slowly open your eyes and connect with your surroundings and others until you are done with the exercise**

CLOSING STEPS

- ▸ **Shake out and stretch your legs**
- ▸ **Makes notes on what you have discovered**

EXERCISE

CLARIFYING VALUES AND
TAKING A PERSONAL OATH

(SEE FULL EXPLANATION OF THIS EXERCISE ON PAGE 50)

PRELIMINARY STEPS

- ▶ **Choose a good time and location**
- ▶ **Start with the basic sitting pose**
- ▶ **Bring your attention to your center**
- ▶ **Place all of your attention on your breath**

MAIN STEPS

- ▶ **Get some paper or a journal and a pen**
- ▶ **Take a look at the following list and read through each item**

VALUES

....

ACCOMPLISHMENT/SUCCESS	**COMPETITION**	**FREEDOM**
ACCOUNTABILITY	**CREATIVITY**	**FRIENDSHIP**
ACCURACY	**DELIGHT IN BEING/JOY**	**FUN**
BEAUTY	**DISCIPLINE**	**HARD WORK**
CALM	**EFFICIENCY**	**INDEPENDENCE**
CHALLENGE	**EQUALITY**	**INNOVATION**
COLLABORATION	**FAITH**	**JUSTICE**
COMMUNITY	**FAMILY**	**KNOWLEDGE**

MASTERING RESPECTFUL CONFRONTATION

LEADERSHIP	PLEASURE	SKILL
LOVE/ROMANCE	POWER	STATUS
LOYALTY	PROSPERITY/WEALTH	TRADITION
MONEY	SERVICE	TRUTH
PEACE/NON-VIOLENCE	SIMPLICITY	WISDOM

....

- ▸ Choose ten values from the list.
- ▸ Choose five values from your list of ten.
- ▸ Choose three values from your list of five.
- ▸ Add them to the empty spaces of the statement below. Once you have filled in the blanks, read the statement to yourself a few times.

"I realize that I have the fortunate circumstances in my life to ensure that I can bring purpose and meaning to my time here on this planet. I will find creative ways to bring about more personal fulfillment and harmony within myself, and empowerment to others, by tapping into my unique abilities and stemming from my core values of _____, _____ and _____."
I commit to living in a way that will create the most positive influence on myself and others, fostering peace, education, generosity, human rights, respect, a healthy environment, and equality for all citizens. I commit to practicing Respectful Confrontation in a skillful and creative way."

CLOSING STEPS

- ▸ Shake out and stretch your legs
- ▸ Make notes on what you have discovered

EXERCISE
GET CENTERED

(SEE FULL EXPLANATION OF THIS EXERCISE ON PAGE 59)

PRELIMINARY STEPS

- ▸ Choose a good time and location
- ▸ Start with the basic sitting pose or the basic standing pose

MAIN STEPS

- ▸ Focus on your center
- ▸ Make this point as concrete as possible
- ▸ Breathe naturally from your center
- ▸ Notice when you stop focusing on your center and return your attention to your center until you are done with the exercise

CLOSING STEPS

- ▸ Shake out and stretch your legs
- ▸ Make notes on what you have discovered

EXERCISE
PRESENCE AND DEEPER LISTENING

(SEE FULL EXPLANATION OF THIS EXERCISE ON PAGE 62)

PRELIMINARY STEPS

- ▸ **Choose a good time and location**
- ▸ **Start with the basic sitting pose**
- ▸ **Bring your attention to your center**
- ▸ **Place all of your attention on your breath**

MAIN STEPS

- ▸ **Become aware of yourself**
- ▸ **Become aware of your surroundings**
- ▸ **Name the things you notice. Continue naming until you are done with the exercise**

CLOSING STEPS

- ▸ **Shake out and stretch your legs**
- ▸ **Make notes on what you have discovered**

EXERCISE

ELEPHANT WALKING

(SEE FULL EXPLANATION OF THIS EXERCISE ON PAGE 75)

PRELIMINARY STEPS

▸ **Choose a good time and location**

▸ **Start with the basic standing pose**

▸ **Bring your attention to your center**

▸ **Place all of your attention on your breath**

MAIN STEPS

▸ **Place foot. Take your first step with no weight in the foot**

▸ **Shift weight into foot**

▸ **Place second foot, no weight in foot**

▸ **Shift weight into foot. Continue**

▸ **Walk forward for one to five minutes**

▸ **Walk sideways for one to five minutes**

▸ **Walk backwards for one to five minutes**

▸ **Walk in all three directions until you are done with the exercise**

CLOSING STEPS

▸ **Shake out and stretch your legs**

▸ **Make notes on what you have discovered**

EXERCISE

"HEY" EXERCISE

(SEE FULL EXPLANATION OF THIS EXERCISE ON PAGE 82)

PRELIMINARY STEPS

- ▸ **Choose a good time and location**
- ▸ **Start with the basic standing pose**
- ▸ **Bring your attention to your center**
- ▸ **Place all of your attention on your breath**

MAIN STEPS

- ▸ **Choose a point across the room**
- ▸ **Pretend to hit it with your force**
- ▸ **Keep repeating the movement**
- ▸ **Make adjustments–Force**
- ▸ **Make adjustments–Precision**
- ▸ **Use your voice with the word "Hey" while doing the movement until you are done with the exercise**

CLOSING STEPS

- ▸ **Shake out and stretch your legs**
- ▸ **Make notes on what you have discovered**

EXERCISE

SELF PORTRAIT OF TRUE POWER

(SEE FULL EXPLANATION OF THIS EXERCISE ON PAGE 102)

PRELIMINARY STEPS

- Choose a good time and location
- Start with the basic sitting pose
- Bring your attention to your center
- Place all of your attention on your breath

MAIN STEPS

- Get some paper or a journal and a pen
- Contemplate your relationship with each power of the Four Pillars of True Power (Grounding, Focus, Strength, Flexibility)—one at a time
- Make notes on what you have discovered about yourself
- Draw yourself as a table
- Label each of the corresponding legs of your table: Grounding, Focus, Strength and Flexibility
- Take a look at your table
- Assess your current situation
- Create a plan of action

CLOSING STEPS

- Shake out and stretch your legs
- Make notes on what you have discovered

EXERCISE

PERSONAL SPACE

(SEE FULL EXPLANATION OF THIS EXERCISE ON PAGE 183)

PRELIMINARY STEPS

▸ Choose a good time and location

▸ Start with the basic standing pose

▸ Bring your attention to your center

▸ Place all of your attention on your breath

MAIN STEPS

▸ Explore the immediate space around you

▸ Explore the space inside of the boundaries of your personal space

▸ Imagine that your personal space is completely sealed off

▸ Close your eyes and feel the comfort and safety within your personal space

▸ Open your eyes again and look out at the world around you from your personal space until you are done with the exercise

CLOSING STEPS

▸ Shake out and stretch your legs

▸ Make notes on what you have discovered

EXERCISE
MAKING CONTACT

(SEE FULL EXPLANATION OF THIS EXERCISE ON PAGE 122)

(SEE FULL EXPLANATION OF THIS EXERCISE ON PAGE 122)

PRELIMINARY STEPS

- ▸ Choose a good time and location
- ▸ Start with either the basic standing or sitting pose
- ▸ Bring your attention to your center
- ▸ Place all of your attention on your breath

MAIN STEPS

- ▸ Connect with the center of your partner, the place of personal power
- ▸ Bring your awareness to your heart, the place of understanding and compassion
- ▸ Connect with the heart of your partner
- ▸ Slowly open your eyes and let you awareness from your center and heart flow to your partner
- ▸ Stay in this connection, noticing how you and the other are influencing each other
- ▸ Practice staying connected and overcoming distractions that break the connection
- ▸ Notice your thoughts and assumptions
- ▸ Put judgments and assumptions aside
- ▸ Stay connected and breathe into the feelings and the energy of this connection until you are done with the exercise

MASTERING RESPECTFUL CONFRONTATION

CLOSING STEPS

Shake out and stretch your legs

Make notes on what you have discovered

Evaluate with your partner

EXERCISE

OUTLINING YOUR CONFRONTATIONS

(SEE FULL EXPLANATION OF THIS EXERCISE ON PAGE 201)

PRELIMINARY STEPS

- ▶ **Choose a good time and location**
- ▶ **Start with the basic sitting pose**
- ▶ **Bring your attention to your center**
- ▶ **Place all of your attention on your breath**

MAIN STEPS

- ▶ **Get some paper or a journal and a pen**
- ▶ **Think of all the people (or aspects of yourself) that you feel you need to confront**
- ▶ **Make a list of these people and personal character traits**
- ▶ **Write the following headlines across the top of another page:**

  NAME | BEHAVIOR | EFFECT | NEED | DESIRED BEHAVIOR | FOLLOW UP

- ▶ **Sort out your notes by filling in the information for each confrontation under the headlines above**
- ▶ **Repeat this process with all the people and personal characters traits on your list**
- ▶ **Practice on your own what you would say, based on the notes you made. First, write it down and then say it out loud many times**

CLOSING STEPS

Shake out and stretch your legs

Make notes on what you have discovered

EXERCISE

FESS UP!

(SEE FULL EXPLANATION OF THIS EXERCISE ON PAGE 225)

PRELIMINARY STEPS

- ▸ Choose a good time and location
- ▸ Start with the basic sitting pose
- ▸ Bring your attention to your center
- ▸ Place all of your attention on your breath

MAIN STEPS

- ▸ Get some paper or a journal and a pen
- ▸ List your own aggressive acts–actions, words, and thoughts
- ▸ Observe others and list their aggressive acts. Do you do them as well?
- ▸ Notice how this makes you feel
- ▸ Write down any decisions you make and any strategies for changing your habits based on what you have discovered

CLOSING STEPS

- ▸ Shake out and stretch your legs
- ▸ Make notes on what you have discovered

PRACTICING NAMING THE BEHAVIOR

(SEE FULL EXPLANATION OF THIS EXERCISE ON PAGE 261)

PRELIMINARY STEPS

- ▶ Choose a good time and location
- ▶ Start with the basic sitting pose
- ▶ Bring your attention to your center
- ▶ Place all of your attention on your breath

MAIN STEPS

- ▶ Get some paper or a journal and a pen
- ▶ Think of all the people (or aspects of yourself) you would like to confront
- ▶ Make a list of the reactive behavior of these people, as well as yourself
- ▶ Group all of the behaviors on your lists under the headings:

FIGHT | FLIGHT | FREEZE

- ▶ Make lists of phrases that will work for you to name behavior
- ▶ Say the statements out loud many times

CLOSING STEPS

- ▶ Shake out and stretch your legs
- ▶ Make notes on what you have discovered

MASTERING RESPECTFUL CONFRONTATION

ABOUT **JOE WESTON**

Joe Weston is renowned in the United States and Europe as a workshop facilitator, a consultant, writer, life coach, creative social activist, and as an advocate for peace. He is the founder and presenter of Respectful Confrontation workshops and lectures.

Weston is a frequent volunteer for the Liberation Prison Project, where he teaches Buddhism to prison inmates. He is also the founder of Heartwalker Studio and the Heartwalker Peace Project, initiating Heartwalks (peace rallies in various cities with routes in the shape of a heart) and peace vigils, thereby creating opportunities for connection, discussion, and creative collaboration.

Born and educated in New York, Weston lived in Amsterdam for seventeen years and now lives in the U.S. He graduated from Hofstra University with an honors degree in Drama and Literature. Weston brings a wealth of insight to his work based on many teachings, including Tai Chi Chuan and a variety of spiritual traditions—plus his extensive experience in theater and organizational trainings. www.joeweston.com

RESPECTFUL CONFRONTATION® WORKSHOPS AND LECTURES

Respectful Confrontation trainings are designed for corporations, organizations, government bodies and for individuals who seek lasting change in the areas of communication, productivity, time and stress management, impactful leadership, empowerment, personal freedom, and fulfillment.

Presented to a clientele around the world, these personal, intensive trainings and private consultations are engines of transformation, resulting in the attainment of true power that leads to self-confidence and peaceful interactions with others.

The Respectful Confrontation experience is unique because it goes beyond theories, incorporating interactive, dynamic exercises and easy-to-apply tools. Participants gain deep insight into themselves and greatly enhanced relationships with others, along with greater ease in tackling challenging situations with integrity and understanding.

Benefits for your company:

- *Enhanced communication skills, increased productivity, and efficiency*
- *Leadership improvement as related to conflict resolution, problem-solving, and relationships with employees*
- *Understanding and implementation of a creative, productive work culture*
- *Team-building and collaboration*
- *Better time and stress management, mediation, and negotiation*

Benefits for the individual:

- *Greater self-confidence, self-expression, and personal freedom*
- *Stronger influence with friends, family, and associates*
- *Enriched relationships, expanded self-awareness*
- *Clarity in personal philosophy, life goals, and vision*
- *Ease in tackling challenging situations and discussions*
- *Inner peace and fulfillment*

Respective Confrontation trainings are offered as weekend workshops, one-day trainings, three-hour seminars, and as lectures. Programs, mediation sessions, and private consultations are designed according to the needs of the client or company. For more information and a schedule of events: www.respectfulconfrontation.com.

NOTES

NOTES

NOTES